The Cubans, Our Footprints Across America

# Fernando Hernandez

# THE CUBANS, OUR FOOTPRINTS ACROSS AMERICA

Alexandria Library

MIAMI

Portada: Emma Vasallo

Tipografía: Pablo Brouwer

www.alexlib.com

## Dedication

I dedicate this book to my adopted homeland, the United States of America. You welcomed and accepted my brother and me along with countless other refugees fleeing a communist dictatorship. For generations many others have travelled far from every corner of the world, escaping political, racial, ethnic, economic, and religious strife and persecution to find in your shores a safe harbor and a new life. I am eternally grateful to the people of this great nation for opening the doors to opportunity, hope, and freedom. But most importantly, for the freedom that we have living in the U.S., may we be vigilant and safeguard it for future generations.

## Acknowledgement

The author wishes to thank and acknowledge the following friends and colleagues for their ideas, suggestions and feedback in the preparation of this book. I am grateful for your invaluable assistance, muchisimas gracias!

María C. González
Manuel (Manny) Gutiérrez
Marta (Cubana Rama) Sosa
Arturo Bueno
Zelde Malevitz
Elena Muller García
Josefina (Fefi) Bacallao
María Del Carmen (Carmencita) Romanach
Maritza Pellon
Lenny Menéndez
José Montes

A special thanks to my dear friend Emma Vasallo, the artist who graciously created the cover of this book.

# Contents

Prologue .............................................................. 13

Introduction ......................................................... 17

Artists/Media/ Entertainers/Authors ........................... 19

Sports Figures ...................................................... 97

Entrepreneurs ...................................................... 121

The Pedro Pan Chapter ............................................ 137

Science/Academia ................................................. 191

Public Servants/Political-Military Figures..................... 235

About the author .................................................. 263

Index ................................................................ 265

# Prologue

Fernando Hernandez has done it again. Very well done. The Cubans, Our Footprints Across America is his second book (the first one was The Cubans, Our Legacy in the United States) devoted to highlight the accomplishments of his fellow Cubans, and Cuban Americans, in the United States. After an extensive research, he has produced this wonderful collection of names and data that includes musicians, writers, performers, playwrights, sculptors, priests, bloggers, journalists, filmmakers, radio and TV personalities, sports figures, entrepreneurs, and more.

The people mentioned in this book are contemporary and alive like Richard Blanco, Carlos Alberto Montaner and Padre Alberto Cutie, or dead, though not forgotten, like Anais Nin and Ana Mendieta. The short, but meticulously researched biographies will give the reader a panoramic view of what Cubans and Cuban Americans have done in the United States for over two centuries.

But The Cubans, Our Footprints Across America isn't just a collective biography or a compilation of cold facts. It contains interesting stories, narrated in an entertaining, fun way. It is full of surprises, too. For example, I wouldn't have suspected, before reading these pages, that a Cuban woman, Lola Sanchez (1844-1895), was a Confederate spy during the Civil War.

A special chapter is devoted to the Pedro Pan children, who left Cuba alone between 1960 and 1962 during Operation Pedro Pan. Many were able to build a successful life in America, after arriving here with no money and no family members. The author, it should be noted, is one of them.

This is a book that makes all Cubans proud. As one of the profiled personalities, Gus Machado, was told when he was a child, "If you got good roots, you have a good chance to make it."

I like to think that we, as Cubans, do tend to have strong roots, so we can make it. This is a must reading for all who call America home.

Teresa Dovalpage, Ph.D., was born in Havana and now lives in Taos, New Mexico where she is a Spanish instructor at UNM Taos. She is also a freelancer for the local newspaper, Taos News. Teresa is a well-known author of six published novels and three collections of short stories.

The United States Census Bureau's 2011 Hispanic population survey reveals that 51, 939, 916 people categorized themselves as Hispanic or Latino. The largest group is composed of those of Mexican origin, 33, 557, 922, followed by Puerto Ricans (4, 885, 294), Cubans (1, 891, 014) and Dominicans (1, 554, 819). Those from Central American roots totaled 4, 623, 170, from South America 3, 071, 280, and other Hispanic or Latino 2, 356, 417. The percentage of the Cuban community within the Hispanic population in the United States is 3.64% as of 2011.

The following data is taken from the 2010 American Community Survey by the Pew Hispanic Center about Hispanics of Cuban Origin:

Immigration status: About 59% of Cubans in the U.S. are foreign born compared with 37% of all Hispanics and 13% of the U.S. population overall. Half of the immigrants from Cuba arrived in the U.S. in 1990 or later. More than half of Cubans (55%) are U.S. citizens.

Language: A majority of (58%) of Cubans speak English proficiently. The other 42% of Cubans ages 5 and older report speaking English less than very well, compared with 35% of all Hispanics.

Age: Cubans are older than the U.S. population and Hispanics as well. The median age of Cubans is 40; the median ages of the U.S. population and all Hispanics are 37 and 27, respectively.

Marital status: Cubans are more likely than Hispanics overall to be married, 46% versus 44%.

Fertility: Less than 6% of Cuban women ages 15 to 44 gave birth in the 12 months prior to this survey. That was less than the rate for all Hispanic women- 8%- and the overall rate for U.S. women- 7%.

Regional dispersion: Cubans are the most geographically concentrated Hispanic origin group. Nearly seven-in-ten (67%) live in Florida.

Educational attainment: Cubans have higher levels of education than the Hispanic population overall. Some 24% of Cubans ages 25 and older-compared with 13% of all Hispanics- have obtained at least a bachelor's degree.

Income: The median annual personal earnings for Cubans ages 16 and older were $25,000 in 2010; the median earnings for all U.S. Hispanics were $20,000.

Poverty status: The share of Cubans who live in poverty, 18%, is similar to that of the general U.S. population (15%) and below the 25% share among all Hispanics.

Health insurance: One quarter of Cubans (25%) do not have health insurance compared with 31% of all Hispanics and 16% of the general U.S. population. Additionally, 10% of Cubans younger than 18 are uninsured.

Homeownership: The rate of Cuban homeownership (57%) is higher than the rate of all Hispanics (47%) but lower than the 65% rate for the U.S. population overall.

# Introduction

This is my second book about the contributions that Cuban immigrants have made in the United States from the 1800s to the present time. In 2012 *The Cubans Our Legacy in the United States* was published by Floricanto Press and made available online through Amazon.com and other online bookstores. Many readers suggested that I needed to expand and include other notable people, subsequently I decided to pen another book under a different title. *The Cubans Our Footprints Across America* does not attempt to portray each and every distinguished Cuban immigrant or the offspring of such immigrants; it is impossible to complete such a task and I apologize to those who wonder, "why isn't so and so profiled?"

I realize that some readers may go straight to the index and, to their dismay, not find the names of well-known Cuban Americans. That's because they are most likely portrayed in the first book. Every person profiled here is new and different from those in the previous work. I do promise that those presented in this book will make for engaging, insightful, provocative, and interesting reading.

## Artists/Media/ Entertainers/Authors

The United States and Cuba have had a long-standing musical relationship that dates many years. The first known Cuban orchestra to play in New York City was Orquesta Vicente Sigler in 1926. Vicente Sigler was a Cuban mulatto who played trumpet and worked with his band in Manhattan hotels. But soon a new orchestra would change forever the music scene.

Don Azpiazu (Justo Angeles Azpiazu 1893-1943) was a leading Cuban orchestra director in the 1920s and 30s. His band introduced authentic Cuban dance music and Cuban musical instruments to a wide audience in the United States. It was his Havana Casino Orchestra which went to New York in 1930, and recorded one of the biggest hits in Cuban music history, The Peanut Vendor (El Manisero). The band included a number of star musicians such as Julio Cueva (trumpet) and singer Antonio Machin.

As noted in the website of Laura May Azpiazu, the band leader's niece, Cuba had already become a popular destination for Americans during the Prohibition in the 1920s, and ties with New York were particular strong. Many influential New York bands regularly played in Havana, and in 1930 Cuban ensemble Don Azpiazu and his Havana Casino Orchestra traveled to New York and recorded the iconic number. It became the first Cuban record to sell more than a million copies and kick-started a Cuban music craze across the United States. Cuban and American music have continued to influence each other ever since. The popularity of the song, based on a *pregon*, a song based on a street vendor's cry, was performed in the *son* style, which combines Spanish guitar and song structure with African rhythms and percussion.

Don Azpiazu's The Peanut Vendor, with its authentically Cuban arrangement, opened the floodgates to other Cuban orchestras and paved the way for future Latin celebrities like Xavier Cugat and Desi Arnaz. Interestingly, despite doom predictions by Guy Lombardo and Walter Winchell ( a New York columnist), the song was a colossal success. Azpiazu demonstrated the enormous commercial potential of Cuban music not only in the U.S., but started a Latin craze in Europe as well. (Preceding information taken from lmazpiazu.com).

Another Cuban bandleader who found fame and fortune in the United States was Jacinto Campillo (1920-2011) better known as Pupi Campo. On December 24, 2011, *The New York Times* published an obituary column about his passing earlier that month at a hospice in Las Vegas.

Pupi Campo found success as a bandleader who brought rippling syncopation to Jack Paar's "The Morning Show" on CBS Television in the early 1950s and to his long career in nightclubs around the country. According to the *Times,* Mr. Campo and his band offered their boisterous Latin sounds on Mr. Paar's show from 1954 to 1956. He was part of a transformation of "The Morning Show" to an entertainment format from news and features; Paar replaced Walter Cronkite as host.

By then Campo had made his name in the nightclub circuit as "the rumba maestro", a name *The New York Daily Mirror* gave him in 1948. After leaving the show, Campo and his band returned to performing at nightclubs, like the Deauville Hotel in Miami, the Paramount and the Chateau Madrid in New York, and Caesars Palace in Las Vegas. The band also performed on Ed Sullivan's 'Toast of the Town" and on 'The Name of the Game". Several Latin musicians who went on to become stars played in Mr. Campo's band, among them Tito Puente, Joe Loco and Cachao Lopez.

Pupi came to New York when he was 20 and was soon performing as a dancer at a Manhattan nightclub. There he met Diosa Costello, a stage actress, whom he married a year later. Through Ms. Costello, Campo met the columnist Walter Winchell, who suggested that he become a bandleader. It was a good idea. In a 2003 review of bands from the past, Latin Beat magazine wrote of "the infernal heat radiated" by the Campo band. Campo was married three times, his second wife was the singer Betty Clooney, Rosemary Clooney's sister; she died in 1976. (Preceding information taken from nytimes.com).

Esteban Fernández is a well-known writer based in Los Angeles, California. At the age of fourteen he began confronting the communist regime in his hometown at a time when most people were terrified of the Castro regime. This forced his parents, afraid of what might happen to their son, to send him into exile at sixteen.

When he was eighteen he enrolled in the Cuban Units of the United States Army, a unit composed of Cuban volunteers who joined the Army. At nineteen he participated in a military expedition against the island where he was caught and imprisoned. After obtaining his freedom he began writing a regular column, La Nota Breve, which was published in the weekly "20 de Mayo". Now thanks to the Internet his writings and opinions reach a wide audience. His poignant and provocative articles about Cuba and Cuban exiles are a must for his faithful readers.

Raúl De Cárdenas, acclaimed playwright, arrived in Miami in 1961 at age 23. At that young age he had written a few plays in Cuba and two had been adapted for television. After spending a few days in Miami, he moved to New York City to start a new life. In 1970 one of his plays, "La Palangana", made its debut in the Duo Theatre in Manhattan. The play was later presented in Los Angeles and Miami.

In the United States Raul has written numerous plays, such as "Recuerdos de Familia"; "Un Hombre al Almanecer" which was awarded with Premio Letras de Oro 1988-1989, University of Miami; "Los Hijos de Ochun"; "El Tiempo es un Acto", and his latest anthology, "Cuatro Obras Escogidas" published by Alexandria Library, Miami, 2010.

"El Pasatiempo Nacional" (there was a reading in New York and Miami) was presented in Oxnard, California. Another of his works "La Ceci", made its debut in New York, then made a run in Puerto Rico and Miami before closing out in New York. "Asi Miami Como en el Cielo" formed his trilogy of plays dealing with homosexuality, homophobia, intolerance and AIDS.

According to noted poet Richard Blanco's webpage, he was born in Cuba, assembled in Spain and imported to the United States- meaning his mother, seven months pregnant, and the rest of the family arrived as exiles from Cuba to Madrid where he was born. Only forty-five days later, the family emigrated once more and settled in New York City, then eventually in Miami where he was raised and educated.

His acclaimed first book of poetry, *City of a Hundred Fires,* explores the yearning and negotiation of cultural identity as a Cuban-American, and received the Agnes Starrett Poetry Prize from the University of Pittsburgh Press. His second book, *Directions to the Beach of the Dead,* won the Beyond Margins Award from the PEN American Center for its continued exploration of the universal themes of cultural identity and homecoming. A third collection, *Looking for the Gulf Motel,* was published by the University of Pittsburgh Press in 2012.

He has been featured on National Public Radio's "All Things Considered", and various conferences and venues including the Miami Book Fair, The Southern Writers Conference, The Sunken Gardens Poetry Festival, the Dodge Poetry Festival, and The Poetry Center at Smith College. Blanco is recipient of two Florida Artist Fellowships, a Residency Fellowship from the Virginia Center for the Creative Arts, and is a John Ciardi Fellow of the Bread Loaf Writers Conference. A builder of cities as well as poems, he holds a Bachelors of Science degree in Civil Engineering and a M.F.A. in Creative Writing.

For President Obama's second swearing-in ceremony in January 21, 2013, Richard Blanco was selected to write and read a poem. Blanco is the first immigrant, Latino and openly gay poet chosen to read at an inauguration and, at 44, also the youngest. He read "One Today", written shortly after the Newton school shooting, the poem references the 20 children killed. (Preceding information taken from richard-blanco.com).

Lucy Arner, a native of Santiago de Cuba, is an active pianist as well as conductor. She began her musical studies at the age of twelve. She attended Baldwin-Wallace College, Indiana University, receiving a Bachelor of Music and a Master of Music degree and continued her doctoral studies at the University of Miami. Currently she is on the faculty of Mannes College of Music and coaches privately in New York City in addition to her busy conducting schedule.

Conductor Arner brings to the podium a special affinity for Italian and French opera that is enhanced by her vast experience working in some of the world's greatest opera houses, such as the Gran Teatre del Liceu in Barcelona and the Metropolitan Opera.

Ms. Arner has conducted opera and concerts all over the world, and was the first woman to conduct opera in Mexico City's historic Palacio de Bellas Artes. She was appointed Artistic Director of the New York Chamber Opera in November 2000, and made her debut with the company conducting an exciting and controversial production of Britten's *Rape of Lucretia*.

On Good Friday of 2010, Ms. Arner conducted the Verdi *Requiem* in Santo Domingo in a nationally televised concert. The year 2011 marked another milestone for Lucy Arner in Miami, as she conducted Florida Grand Opera's

*The Tales of Hoffmann* for her debut with the company, and received the Henry C. Clark Conductor Award for the 2010-2011 season. ( Preceding information taken from lucyarner.com).

Manuel Carbonell (October 25, 1918- November 19, 2011) was known as one of the last Cuban master sculptors. An article by Christine Dolen in *The Miami Herald* chronicles his fascinating life as a world class artist. One of his monumental works, The Pillar of History, a 53 foot bronze monument to the Tequesta Indians, is located off the Brickell Avenue Bridge in downtown Miami. The Cuban-born sculptor was also known for the Carbonell Awards, honoring theater artists in South Florida for more than three decades.

Carbonell belonged to a select group of Cuban master sculptors that included Wilfredo Lam and Augustin Cardenas. He began his studies at Havana's Escuela Nacional de Bellas Artes in 1937. Ms. Dolen notes that a serious fall at the age of 18 cost him a kidney and left him paralyzed for a year, the first of several medical crises that would affect or influence his art. He graduated as a professor of drawing and sculpture in 1945 and began his life as an artist. His first international award was in 1954 from Barcelona's III Bienal Hispanoamericana de Arte, for *Fin de una raza* (End of a Race), Carbonell's Capellania stone sculpture of a Taino Indian woman.

The article highlights that he was a rising star in Cuba, interviewing artists on a weekly television show, launching an interior design company for which he created furniture, travelling through Europe where the work of Impressionist and Abstract artists began to influence his own work. In 1959 he left Cuba, his work and family, arriving in New York with $200 to his name. By 1963, he had the first of seven one-man shows at Manhattan's Schoneman Gallery on Madison Avenue, where his work was shown for a dozen years. Gradually he brought his family to the United States; first his two nephews and sisters, in 1974 Carbonell relocated his studio to Miami to be close to his family.

In 1975 he got involved in the theater community when he was asked by Bill Von Maurer, the late *Miami News* theatre and arts critic, to design an award statue honoring the best work in theatre from each season by the South Florida Critics' Circle. Carbonell agreed, shaped the circle into a graceful egg, and the awards were renamed the Carbonells in his honor. His legacy endures all over the world; from a park in Shanghai to the Gerald R. Ford presidential museum in Michigan.

Some of his other works include the monument El Centinela Del Rio; a 21-foot bronze and alabaster sculpture located at Tequesta Point in Brickell Key, Miami. He also created the 15-foot piece Horse and Rider which Burt Reynolds commissioned for his former theater. Another sculpture Amantes, graces the entrance of the Hotel Bristol in the Republic of Panama. Grateful to the U.S., he presented in 1976 at a formal ceremony at the Rose Garden in the White House his Bicentennial Eagle as his gift to the United States of America which is now part of the Smithsonian Collection at the Gerald Ford Museum. He continued working into his 90s in his studio in Miami. Dr. Fred Schoneman, Director of the former renowned Schoneman Galleries, said in 1974; "Carbonell is one of the Masters of Sculpture of our time".

Although not an artist or celebrity, the following person certainly made news. Vivian Lousie Illing was the oldest living survivor of the 1906 San Francisco earthquake; she died on January 22, 2009. An obituary dated January 27, 2009 in *The San Francisco Chronicle* notes that she was born in West Newton, Massachusetts, on Christmas Day 1900, she moved with her family to San Francisco in 1903. She was the third of four children of Juan Rego de Cora of Spain and Elvira Martinez de Pedroso of Havana. A pattern of long life in her family was established by one of her ancestors, Diego de Sotolongo, who came to Cuba in 1517 and died there at 94, the oldest man on the island.

Illing attended public schools in San Francisco and was active in women's clubs, gardening and reading. She entertained many generations with her vivid memories of the earthquake and the 1915 Panama Pacific Exposition. Famous for her good cheer, quick wit and broad cultural interests, she was a remarkable personality who left a fondly indelible imprint on all who had the good fortune to know her.

Author and journalist Carlos Alberto Montaner was born in Havana in 1943. He has written more than 25 books and thousands of articles, including several novels, the last of which is *La mujer del coronel* or *The colonel's wife*. PODER magazine has estimated that more than six million readers have access to his weekly columns. Montaner is a political analyst for CNN in Spanish and a collaborator of the book *The Cuban Exile*, along with well-known Cuban writers Mirta Ojito, and award-winning poet and writer Carlos Eire, a book coordinated by Cuban musician and producer Emilio Estefan. In October 2012 Foreign Policy magazine selected Montaner as one of the fifty most influential intellectuals in the Iberoamerican world.

As a young man living in the early days of the Cuban Revolution, Montaner was arrested on charges of terrorism, an accusation he vehemently denied. He was imprisoned but managed to escape and in 1970 he relocated to Spain from the United States. In 2007 the government of the Comunidad de Madrid awarded the Prize for Tolerance to Montaner, a distinction that is given to those who have fought for the freedom and respect for human rights.

After earning a Master's degree from the University of Miami, Montaner taught American Literature at the Interamerican University of Puerto Rico from 1966 to 1970. During this time he began writing a weekly column which was soon appearing in almost every Latin American country, often in the most widely read newspapers. He also came to be much in demand as a lecturer throughout the hemisphere, speaking about the defense of liberty, economic development, and the important role of culture in the evolution of societies.

In the 1980s, Montaner began a weekly television commentary that was aired by satellite through Latin America. He also produced three books, one of which was *Fidel Castro y la revolucion cubana*, subsequently published in English, Italian and Russian. In 1980 he received the ABC prize for journalism, awarded by the then Spanish premier Adolfo Suarez. By then, his columns were being published in a number of newspapers in the United States, and *The Miami Herald* invited him to join its Editorial Board. Since 2004 he writes weekly columns published in English. He also edited the opinion page of *El Nuevo Herald* between 1987 and 1989. The best-selling *Manual del Perfecto Idiota Lationamericano,* in which he collaborated with Alvaro Vargas Llosa and Plinio Apuleyo Mendoza, was published in 1996 and in English in 2000.

Félix González-Torres (1957-1996) was a Cuban-born visual artist. He was known for his minimal installations and sculptures in which he used materials such as strings of light bulbs, clocks, stacks of paper, or packaged hard candies. Gonzalez-Torres's 1992 piece "Untitled" (Portrait of Marcel Brient) sold for $4.6 million at Phillips de Pury & Company in 2010, a record for the artist at auction.

He was raised in Puerto Rico where he graduated from the Colegio San Jorge in 1976 and began his art studies at the University of Puerto Rico while actively participating in the local art scene. He would later earn a BFA in Photography from the Pratt Institute of Art in New York in 1983. In 1987, he was awarded a Masters of Fine Arts degree by the International Center of Photography and New York University. Subsequently he taught at New York University and briefly at the California Institute of the Arts in Valencia. In 1992 Gonzalez-Torres was granted a DAAD fellowship to work in Berlin, and in 1993 a fellowship from the National Endowment for the Arts.

Gonzalez-Torres was considered within his time to be a process artist due to the nature of his removable installations by which the process is a key feature to the installation. Many of his installations invite the viewer to take a piece of the work with them; a series of works allow viewers to take packaged candies from a pile in the corner of an exhibition space and, in so doing, contribute to the slow disappearance of the sculpture over the course of the exhibit.

One of his most recognizable works "Untitled" (1991), was a billboard installed in twenty-four locations throughout New York City of a monochrome photograph of an unoccupied bed, made after the death of his long-time partner, Ross Laycock, from AIDS. In 2011, "Untitled" (Aparicion), 1991, a stack of endlessly replenishable paper, each sheet printed with a black and white image of clouds, was sold well over the estimate for $1.6 million at Sotheby's, New York. One of the artist's plastic beads pieces, "Untitled" (Blood), was sold for $1.65 million at Christine's, New York, in 2000.

Rita de Acosta Lydig (born Rita Hernandez de Alba de Acosta, 1875-1929) was a unique and colorful character who was emblematic of the excesses in certain social circles in the early part of the 20th century. She was an American socialite regarded as the most picturesque woman in America. Rita was photographed by Adolf de Meyer, Edward Steichen, and Gertrude Kasebier, sculpted in alabaster by Malvina Hoffman, and was painted by Giovanni Boldini and John Singer Sargent, among others. She also wrote one novel, *Tragic Mansions*, under the name Mrs. Philip Lydig, a society melodrama described as emotionally moving and appealing by *The New York Times*.

Rita de Acosta was born in New York City in 1875 to Ricardo de Acosta, a steam-line executive of Cuban descent and a Spanish mother, Micaela Hernandez de Alba y de Alba, reputedly a relation of the Dukes of Alba. On January 3, 1895, aged 19, she became the first wife of William Earl Dodge Stokes, a multimillionaire with whom she had a son. The marriage was troubled and when it was dissolved in 1900, she received a settlement of nearly two million dollars, a record for the time. In 1902 she married Captain Philip M. Lydig, a retired officer in the United States Army. They separated in 1914 and divorced in 1919.

In 1921 Lydig announced her engagement to Rev. Percy Stickney Grant, rector of the Church of the Ascension. But the wedding plans were broken off in 1924 when the bishop refused to authorize the marriage, citing Lydig being a divorcee with two living former husbands. Rev. Grant died shortly afterwards, leaving his personal fortune to the woman he had hoped to marry, and Lydig spent large sums of money on fashion, art, furniture, and other objects to overcome her grief. Heavily in debt, she was forced to sell her home and its contents, was declared bankrupt, and died of pernicious anemia at the age of 54.

Famous for her extravagant lifestyle, Rita was equally welcomed in Paris, where she spent parts of each year. She would arrive at the Ritz with a hairdresser, masseuse, chauffeur, secretary, maid and forty Louis Vuitton trunks. In Paris, she joined ranks with musicians, artists, intellectuals, and philosophers, names like Rodin, Eleonora Duse, Yvette Guilbert and others. Lydig lived in New York, Paris and London and counted Edgar Degas, Leo Tolstoy, Sarah Bernhardt, Ethel Barrymore and Claude Debussy among her friends. Her personal wardrobe became the basis for the start of the Costume Institute at the Metropolitan Museum of Art. She is buried with her mother and sister Mercedes at Trinity Church Cemetery in New York City.

Alberto R. Cutie is an Episcopal cleric better known as Padre Alberto. He was born in Puerto Rico of Cuban parents in 1969. Cutie was ordained a Catholic priest of the Roman Catholic Church in 1995 and became an internationally recognizable name by hosting television and radio programs.

Cutie left the Catholic Church in May 2009 after publication of photographs showing him embracing a woman in the sand in Miami Beach, and his subsequent admission that he was in love. He has said that mandatory celibacy was only one of the theological differences that led him to leave Catholicism for the Episcopal Church. After he requested a leave of absence from his duties in the Archdiocese of Miami, Cutie married Ruhama Buni Canellis, and joined the Episcopal Church. Cutie currently serves as Rector at an Episcopal parish in Biscayne Park, a community near Miami. He was received as a Episcopal priest on May 29, 2010.

The reverend has a long career in radio and television as "Father Albert", he was the first priest to host a secular talk show both on radio and television. He is also a regular columnist whose writings appear in many Spanish language newspapers throughout the United States and Latin America. He gained worldwide recognition with his television debut in 1999 as the host of *Padre Alberto* (and later *Cambia tu vida con el Padre Alberto*), a daily talk show televised on the Telemundo network. He later served as host of the weekly program *America en Vivo* on Telemundo International.

Beginning in 2002, Cutie hosted a weekly talk program called *Hablando claro con el Padre Alberto*, reaching millions of households throughout the United States, Canada, Spain and Latin America on EWTN Español. In July 2003 he officiated at singer Celia Cruz's funeral Mass in Miami. The highly popular Cutie has been labeled as "Father Oprah" by various publications.

On January 4, 2011, Father Albert released his new candid memoir, *Dilemma*. With the release of his new book he has appeared on *Good Morning America*, *The View*, *Fox and Friends*, *The Joy Behar Show*, as well as several national Spanish language television programs including *Don Francisco Presenta*, *Despierta America* and *Al Rojo Vivo*. While some claim the book is harsh on the Catholic Church, Father Cutie has explained that he did not write it with that intention. He has repeatedly said, "This is not an attack on the Church, but a memoir about my personal experience of 25 years as a young man discerning, preparing and living in the Catholic priesthood".

Marta Sosa, widely known as Cubana Rama of radio fame, is a Havana native. The popular blog radio personality came to the United States along with her family and settled in Union City, New Jersey, a city with a sizeable Cuban-American population. Marta attended and graduated from Union Hill High School.

Her family relocated to Minnesota in 1976 seeking better employment opportunities. In Minneapolis Cubana Rama held many jobs in the financial sector of downtown Minneapolis but once she married and had her first child, she decided to change careers to spend more time with her son Alexander. Marta started working as a cosmetologist, a profession she loved from childhood but soon she realized that she needed more education and skills, subsequently she enrolled in college, earning a degree in Journalism from Augsburg College in Minneapolis.

With the advent of social media and the Internet, Marta quickly sought old friends from Cuba and New Jersey. With the help of Facebook she achieved both. One of her old schoolmates suggested that she host a radio program on the Internet, and this sparked her interest in creating Cubana Rama Talk Radio.

In 2009, Marta launched the Cubana Rama Talk Radio inviting guests from all over the world providing them a platform to communicate like never before. Her initial following from New Jersey, New York, Miami, California, and the Midwest has grown to Latin America and Europe. She hosts programs in both English and Spanish to her growing audience; Cubana Rama also hosted a program featuring missing persons in the USA, but once families of victims abroad heard the show, they too asked her to assist them in bringing attention to this growing problem. Marta loves hosting her blog radio program and enjoys getting to know the hearts of women and men behind the stories she features. The theme song of her blog radio program paints an accurate picture of Marta/Cubana Rama; her legions of followers know that she is one persona, in other words, Marta Sosa and Cubana Rama are inseparable personalities and entities. What you hear is what she is, and that's one of the reasons for her popularity. There is nothing orchestrated or fake about her show or person.

Manolo de Jesus Reyes Xigues, J.D. (1924-2008), better known as Manolo Reyes, was a Cuban-American Spanish-language television news broadcaster in Miami, Florida. Reyes became a television pioneer in the 1960s when he became one of South Florida's first Spanish-language newscasters. His first 15 minute news shows, *News En Español*, debuted on WTVJ on August 28, 1960 at 6:45 am at a time when Spanish-language broadcasts were rare in the Miami metropolitan area. His original broadcasts were aimed at making news accessible to the growing Spanish-speaking, Miami-based Cuban exile community.

Reyes, who resided in the Miami area in the 1950s and 1960s, realized that there were no television news shows aimed at the exile community. Despite his limited English, he pitched his idea to the founder of WTVJ, Mitchell Wolfson, and Miami television pioneer Ralph Renick. They both agreed to let Reyes tape a test program. The station had to have the test show critiqued by a University of Miami linguistics professor because no one at WTVJ (Channel 4) spoke Spanish at the time.

Wolfson agreed to broadcast Reyes' Spanish-language news segments. *News En Español* aired on weekdays at 6:45 am, just before the *Skipper Chuck Show*, and at 1 am, just before the station's sign-off for the night. Spanish-speaking viewers, especially the Cuban exile community, were delighted by the news show, despite the difficult viewing times. Conversely, non-Spanish speakers were equally outraged by the broadcast of an all-Spanish program.

Reyes' newscast was so popular that it was gradually expanded. His initial assignments for the station involved coverage of Miami's arriving Cuban refugees. He remained at WTVJ for 19 years and was promoted to the station's Latin America news editor. Reyes also became a regular contributor on WTVJ's well-known English-language show *The Ralph Renick Report*. He also began contributing nationally on Walter Cronkite's *CBS Evening News*.

After leaving television he obtained a second law degree at age 52 from the University of Miami before becoming an executive director at Mercy Hospital in Miami. He remained at that position for nearly 20 years until his retirement in 2005. Reyes was honored for his pioneering work in television by the Miami Chapter of the National Academy of Television Arts and Sciences in 1991. He founded a number of Miami community organizations including the YMCA Jose Marti, the Cuban Sertoma Club, and the Spanish Post of Veterans of Foreign Wars. He also served on the board of directors of several organizations, including the Hialeah-Miami Springs Chamber of Commerce, Easter Seals, the United Way and Barry University. He was honored with an Emmy Award for Broadcast Journalism, Keys to the City of Hialeah and Key West, the Pentagon Award for Human Goals, the Archbishop Hurley Award, and many others.

Marta Maria Darby is a popular social media personality, widely known for her blog, My Big, Fat, Cuban Family. Marta categorizes herself as a designer, blogger, Cuban cook, scrapbooker, photographer, wife, and mother of four. She has been blogging for almost six years-sharing her life, culture, family, and recipes in her own Cuban-American style. She loves to tell stories of her extraordinarily ordinary Cuban-American life.

So, who is this intriguing blogger that has so many converts? She was born in Havana and left Cuba on February 14th, 1961. She states that all of her family's memories of Cuba, B.C. (Before Castro) are happy ones. They still maintain many of their Cuban traditions, particularly the music and food. Her parents, Luz and Rodolfo Verdes, served as role models as they were married for 60 years. Today Marta and her husband Eric make their home in Southern California.

Her blog, My Big, Fat, Cuban Family, is a daily destination for hundreds, if not, thousands of Cubans worldwide. Every day she gets to weave stories and anecdotes about her very passionate and fabulous Cuban family and the ever-present Cuban food. She gets to celebrate the blending of her two defining cultures as she lives life on the Cuban-American hyphen. Marta considers herself 100% Cuban and 100% American.

Marta's Cuban-American Kitchen was born online 5 years ago when she was invited to become a regular contributor to the popular exile blog, Babalu Blog. She considers herself pretty masterful at taking the Cuban recipes that she grew up with and re-inventing them for today's modern kitchen. Rumors abound that she also makes a mean all-American apple pie. In 2009, along with her online partner and friend, Carrie Ferguson Weir, she helped launch the popular Latina Cultural site, Tiki Tiki Blog. Many of her stories, recipes, and videos can be found populating those pages.

Pedro Gómez is a Phoenix-based reporter for ESPN's *Sportscenter* show. He is primarily a baseball reporter and is also a member of the Baseball Writers Association of America. He has covered 15 World Series, and more than 10 All-Star Games and is a voting member for the Baseball Hall of Fame.

Gomez is the son of Cuban refugees, born just 20 days after his parents arrived in 1962, two months before the missile crisis of October 1962. He attended Miami-Dade

Community College and the University of Miami. After years of covering high schools and general assignment sports in Miami, San Diego and the San Francisco Bay area, Gomez became a full-time baseball beat writer in 1992, covering the Oakland Athletics for *The San Jose Mercury News* and *Sacramento Bee* from 1990 to 1997.

During his tenure as a writer covering the Athletics, Gomez, a lifetime baseball fan, covered major topics such as the Cincinnati Reds victory over the defending World Series champion A's in 1990, Jose Canseco's trade to the Texas Rangers for Ruben Sierra in 1992, Ricky Henderson's 1,000th stolen base, and other moments of relative importance to the team.

His work in Sacramento, San Jose and later as a national baseball writer and general sports columnist for *The Arizona Republic* in Phoenix from 1997 to 2003 led to ESPN's hiring him in 2003 to work at *Sportscenter*.

Maria Canals Barrera is a Miami native of Cuban/Catalan/American origin. She is an actress, voice actress and singer. She is best known for her roles as Theresa Russo in *Wizards of Waverly Place*, Connie Torrs in *Camp Rock* and *Camp Rock2: The Final Jam*, and as the voice of Shayera Hol/Hawkgirl in *Justice League* and *Justice League Unlimited*. She also voiced the character of Sunset in the Disney Channel show, *The Proud Family*.

She has worked extensively in theatre in both Miami and Los Angeles. She made her network television debut in the 1993 TV series *Key West* and has appeared in the WB series *Popular* as a prostitute by the name of Candybox, as well as such films as *America's Sweethearts*, and *The Master of Disguises*. Among her recent awards are four Imagen

Awards for "Best Supporting Actress: Television" in 2008, 2009, 2010, and 2011; in 2009 she earned the ALMA Award for "Actress in Television-Comedy" and in 2011 another ALMA Award for "Favorite TV Actress-Supporting Role".

Alex Abella arrived from Cuba in 1961 at age 11. His family settled in New York where he attended Columbia University on a Pulitzer scholarship. He is a journalist and author best known for his non-fiction works *Soldiers of Reason: The RAND Corporation and the Rise of the American Empire (2008)* and *Shadow Enemies: Hitler's Secret Terrorist Plot Against the United States* (2003, with Scott Gordon).

After college Abella moved to California to work for *The San Francisco Chronicle* initially covering local news, then network news as a reporter, writer, and producer. In the late 1980s Abella went to Los Angeles, spending seven years as a Spanish language interpreter for the Los Angeles Superior Court. His first novel, *The Killing of the Saints* (1991), is a Los Angeles thriller about the beliefs of the Santeria religion used as a defense for murder. *Saints* and its sequels, *Dead of Night* (1998) and *Final Act* (2000), feature a Cuban-American lawyer and investigator of Cuban origin.

Abella's second novel, *The Great American* (1997), is set in Cuba in 1957 during the Cuban Revolution and is a fictionalized story of a United States Marine who fought on the side of Fidel Castro. Abella's non-fiction work includes *Shadow Enemies: Hitler's Secret Terrorist Plot Against the United States* (2003), co-authored with law professor and current Los Angeles Superior Court judge Scott Gordon. The book is set in Germany during World War II and follows a group of German-American agents trained in sabotage and terrorism. His book, *Soldiers of Reason: The RAND Corporation and the Rise of the American Empire* (2008), is the first history of the foreign policy think tank founded by the U.S. Military and partly funded by the United States government.

In addition to his non-fiction books, he has been a contributing writer with *The Los Angeles Times* and now contributes to the *Huffington Post*. At KTVU-TV, Abella was nominated for an Emmy Award for "Best Breaking News Story". His first novel, *The Killing of the Saints* (1991), was a *New York Times* Notable Book.

Liz Balmaseda is a Pulitzer Prize-winning journalist who writes for *The Palm Beach Post*. She was born in Puerto Padre, Cuba during the Cuban Revolution and she grew up in Miami. She received an Associate's degree from Miami-Dade Community College, and then a Bachelor's degree from Florida International University in Communications in 1981.

She had been an intern for *The Miami Herald* in 1980, and was hired upon her graduation to write for *El Herald*, *The Miami Herald's* Spanish-language sister newspaper. Balmaseda worked in this and several other reporting assignments at the *Herald* until 1985, when she left to become Central America bureau chief, based in El Salvador, for *Newsweek*. She moved to NBC News as a field producer based in Honduras before returning to *The Miami Herald* in November 1987 as a feature writer.

Balmaseda was awarded her first Pulitzer Prize for Commentary in 1993 for her writings on the plight of Cuban and Haitian refugees. Her second was awarded for breaking-news reporting in 2001, for her role in covering the story of Elian Gonzalez. That same year, she won the Hispanic Heritage Award for Literature.

Alfredo Alonso is a Cuban-born media executive. He joined Clear Channel Radio in August 2004 as Senior Vice President-Hispanic Radio. He is responsible for leading Clear Channel Radio's Spanish-language radio initiatives, including expanding the availability of Spanish-language programming into markets of all sizes. Since he assumed the position CCR has converted 30 stations in 25 markets. Additionally, Alonso was the innovator of the MEGA bilingual/bicultural format, expanded La Preciosa Network to 21 affiliates and established Spanish formats for HD2 and Premium choice applications. Many of the stations converted over the last five years have become format leaders in their respective markets while posting gains in overall revenue versus prior formats.

Prior to joining CCR, Alonso was Vice Chairman of Mega Communications LLC, from September 2002 to November 2003. He served as President and Chief Executive Officer/Limited Partner of the 20 Spanish radio group from November 1998 to September 2002. Alonso founded Mega Broadcasting LLC, in August, 1996, and served as President and Chief Financial Officer until selling the group in November 1998. The company owned and operated stations in Philadelphia, Hartford, Washington, D.C., and Tampa. He served as Vice President and General Manager of Spanish Broadcasting System, Inc. from April 1993 to August 1996.

Alonso also managed daily operations for WSKQ-FM, WPAT-FM and WSKQ-AM in New York. He also created the "Mega" format concept and repositioned WSKQ into

Mega 97.9, which became a top Arbitron ranked station. Prior to fulltime employment with Spanish Broadcasting, he consulted in the creation of the "La X" format concept and consulted KLAX/Los Angeles during its run as the number one station in that market.

Alonso has extensive experience in reaching and serving the Hispanic radio industry. He founded and operated the premier Spanish-language weekly radio trade newspaper, Radio Y Musica, serving as Publisher/President from January 1990 to March 2000. In March 2000 Alonso sold the company to Radio & Records.

Valerie Cruz is an actress born in Elizabeth, New Jersey of Cuban origin. She attended Florida State University and earned a BFA Theatre degree. She has appeared in films such as *Cellular* and played Grace Santiago in *Nip/Tuck*, but she left the show just after one season. She has made guest appearances in series such as *Grey's Anatomy* and *Las Vegas*. In 2007, she appeared as Connie Murphy, a tough Chicago police detective, in SciFi Channel's adaptation of *The Dresden Files*.

She has also played Maria Nolan on the CW's *Hidden Palms*. In 2008, she appeared in season three of *Dexter*, playing Sylvia Prado, the wife of Assistant District Attorney Miguel Prado (Jimmy Smits). In 2009, she appeared in the horror film *The Devil's Tomb* and the HBO series *True Blood*, in which she played the part of Isabel. That same year she played Olivia in the film *La Linea*. In 2010 she became part of the cast of the ABC drama *Off the Map*, which was cancelled by ABC on May 13, 2011. In 2011 she had a recurring role as a Homeland Security agent in the Syfy series *Alphas*. In 2012, she played a doctor in the "Organ

Grinder" episode of *Grimm*; the wife of a dictator in the "Enemy of the State" episode of *Scandal*; and an investigator for the football league in the episode "Spell It Out" of *Necessary Roughness*. Cruz received a 2008 Alma Awards Nomination; Best Lead Actress in a drama series for *The Dresden Files* on SciFi Channel; she also received a 2009 Screen Actors Guild Award Nomination; Best Ensemble Cast in a drama series for *Dexter* on Showtime Network.

Ambrose E. Gonzáles (1857-1926) was not only an illustrious journalist, but a businessman who, against tremendous odds, kept afloat and saw flourish *The State* newspaper, which he and his brother, N.G. Gonzáles, founded. Ambrose Elliott Gonzales was born May 27, 1857, in Paulo Parish, South Carolina, the son of General Ambrosio Jose and Harriet Rutledge Elliott Gonzales. His father was a brilliant and adventurous Cuban revolutionary general who battled the oppressive rule of Spain.

Jobless and broke after the American Civil War, his father tried several unsuccessful enterprises, including farming at devastated Oak Lawn, the family's plantation. He took his family to Cuba in 1869 to accept a college teaching position. However, his wife contracted yellow fever and died after a short illness. After her death, the general returned with his six children to Charleston, South Carolina where they were reared by their grandmother and their mother's two sisters.

Educated mostly at home, Ambrose managed brief stints in private schools in Virginia, Charleston, and Beaufort, where he showed his business acumen by buying and selling poultry, cutting crossties for sale, and tending to matters at his family's plantation ruins.

In 1891, Ambrose and N.F. Gonzales founded *The State* as an outspoken Columbia daily newspaper. In 1893, Ambrose became business manager, president, treasurer, and general manager of The State Company, as well as publisher of the newspaper. He retained these positions until his death.

The controversial enterprise struggled at first. It taxed Ambrose Gonzales' considerable financial skills to keep it going while his brothers, N.G. and William Elliott Gonzales, concentrated on the news and editorial pages. N.G. Gonzales died January 19, 1903, four days after being shot by the lame-duck lieutenant governor, James Tillman, across the street from the State House. The day after his brother's death, Gonzales ended a signed editorial with the words, "With heavy hearts his work is taken over by those who loved him well, and in his name *The State* is pledged anew to the principles for which he gave his life".

Gonzales never lost his interest in writing. He made a unique and lasting contribution with his famous sketches employing the Gullah dialect (a creole language spoken by the Gullah people, an African-American population living on the Sea Islands and the coastal region of North and South Carolina, Georgia, and Northeast Florida); he devoted 35 years to the growth and health of the newspaper, which became the state's largest.

The fiery William Watts Ball who served as acting editor of *The State* and later of the *News and Courier*, in 1932 wrote that Gonzales was "the most important and greatest South Carolinian since Governor Hampton, though South Carolinians do not yet know it". Gonzales was inducted in the South Carolina Business Hall of Fame in 1986, 60 years after his death. (Preceding information taken from www. knowitall.org).

Award-winning filmmaker Amy Serrano produced, wrote, and directed the feature-length and critically acclaimed documentary, "The Sugar Babies: The Plight of the Children of Agricultural Workers on the Sugar Industry of the Dominican Republic". The Cuban-born filmmaker's work explores the lives of the descendants of the first Africans delivered to the island of Hispaniola for the bittersweet commodity that once ruled the world. These very same people continue to be trafficked from Haiti to the Dominican Republic to work on sugar plantations under circumstances that can only be considered modern day slavery.

While based in Miami, Amy also wrote, produced and directed the U.S. co-production for the feature-length film "MOVE!". Produced in Rome, Italy and distributed throughout film festivals in Europe, "MOVE!" is a fictional film composed of short films by 11 filmmakers in 6 continents exploring the dispassionate state of humanity through varied human emotions.

Her body of work includes directing and producing the PBS broadcast "A Woman's Place: Voices of Contemporary Hispanic-American Women", featuring Isabel Allende, Dr. Antonia Novello, Bianca Jagger, Maria Hinojosa, Esmeralda Santiago, Marjorie Agosin and other barrier breaking Hispanic-American women. Amy also produced the award-winning "Adios Patria? The Cuban Exodus" narrated by Andy Garcia (Berlin Film Festival, Best Documentary New York Independent Film and Video Festival, PBS). She executive produced the PBS broadcast and

Emmy-award nominated "Café con Leche: Voices of Exiles' Children" and associate produced the Emmy-award nominated "Havana: Portrait of Yesterday", narrated by Gloria Estefan for PBS.

In June of 2003, Amy became a recipient of the Tesoro Award in Art and Culture. In January of 2004, she was awarded a prestigious Fellowship in the National Hispanic Leadership Institute that has involved Leadership Studies at Harvard University's JFK School of Government, the Center for Creative Leadership, on Capital Hill and with various recognized leaders in social and civic posts.

In July of 2004, she was named a "Latina of Excellence" in Hispanic Magazine's Top Latinas Roster for 2004. In July of 2005, she was named one of fifteen top Young Hispanic Leaders in the U.S. by the Spanish Embassy in Washington, D.C. In 2006, she was selected to be profiled in the Florida Hispanic Yearbook. In May of 2008, MEGA TV named her "one of the most influential and recognized Hispanics in the U.S." and in October 2009, she was selected as a "Mujer Vanidades" in Vanidades Magazine.

Amy has just released a book of poetry entitled "Of Fiery Places and Sacred Spaces" and is directing an interdisciplinary multiplatform initiative exploring the meaningful impact of place upon identity. She is also engaged in producing a multimedia project that will involve a film, a book and traveling photo installation centering on the human rights of children. A poet, writer, essayist and speaker of four languages, she remains a Senior Fellow of the Human Rights Foundation in New York, serves on the board of Culture in the City in Miami; is a Fellow of the National Hispanic Leadership in Washington, D.C.; is on the Advisory Council Member of the Faulkner Society in New Orleans. Amy was recently appointed a founding Board Member to Ambassador Armando Valladares' non-governmental organization, Human Rights for All. (Preceding information taken from www.amyserrano.com).

Dan Le Batard is a newspaper sportswriter, radio host, and television reporter based out of Miami, Florida. He is best known for his work in his hometown paper, *The Miami Herald*, for whom he has worked since 1990. Since 2004, he has also hosted his own radio show, *The Dan Le Batard Show with Stugotz*, on a local Miami radio station. He is a frequent contributor to several ESPN programs, serving as a regular replacement host for *Pardon the Interruption* when one of the regular hosts is out. In 2011, he began hosting the ESPN2 show *Dan Le Batard is Highly Questionable* with his father, Gonzalo Le Batard, whom he calls "papi".

Le Batard was born in Jersey City (a city with a sizeable Cuban-American population) New Jersey; Dan's brother is Miami-based artist, David Le Batard, professionally known as LEBO. Dan graduated from the University of Miami in 1990 with a B.A. in Journalism and Politics. During his college career, he was a sportswriter for the college newspaper, *The Miami Hurricane*. While at the U, he received criticism for helping to escalate the rancor in the UM versus University of Notre Dame football rivalry by publishing Lou Holtz's personal phone number and by referring to coach Lou Holts as Sir Lou or Lou Sir (Loser). He requested his readers to call all thorough the week of the game to help distract the coach. Le Batard prides himself as being the "uncomfortable" sports journalist. He often writes about controversial topics, especially race. He is a recurring guest on *Outside the Lines*, *The Sports Reporters*, and *College GameDay*.

Melinda López is a noted playwright and performer who is also a faculty member in Theatre Studies at Wellesley College in Massachusetts. The Cuban American took a rather long journey before reaching New England; her parents left Cuba and she was born in Cali, Colombia before arriving in the U.S. as a young girl. She graduated with a B.A. from Dartmouth College and earned a M.A. from Boston University.

She is the author of *Caroline in Jersey* (Williamstown Theatre Festival), *Sonia Flew* (Elliot Norton Award "Best New Play"), *Irne* ("Best Play", "Best Production", Huntington Theatre, Steppenwolf, Coconut Grove Playhouse, Laguna Playhouse, NPR, et.al.), *Gary* (Steppenwolf First Look Repertory, Boston Playwrights Theatre), *Alexandros* (Laguna Playhouse), and a translation of *Blood Wedding*, (Suffolk University).

Her other award-winning plays include *God Smells Like a Roast Pig* (Women on Top Festival, Elliot Norton Award "Outstanding Solo Performance"), *Midnight Sandwich/Medianoche* (Coconut Grove Playhouse), *The Order of Things* (CentaStage, Kennedy Center Fund for New Plays), *How Do You Spell Hope?* (Underground Railway Theatre). Melinda is also an actress, appearing in regional theatres across the country, and has worked in film and radio.

Melinda was the first recipient of the Charlotte Woolard Award, given by the Kennedy Center to a "promising new voice in American Theatre". She volunteers with New Voices: Young Playwrights Project, which teaches playwriting to underserved communities. She is also active in the Cuban American community of Boston, and helps with local charities. The multi-talented writer has also completed two marathons; she loves back country hiking, anything to do with the southwest American desert, and sneaking into movie matinees on rainy days with her daughter. ( Preceding information taken from new. wellesley.edu).

Antonio Sacre is a bilingual storyteller, author and performance artist. He was born in Boston to an Irish-American mother and a Cuban father. Sacre earned a B.A. in English from Boston College and a M.A. in Theatre Arts from Northwestern University. He has performed at the National Book Festival at the Library of Congress, the Kennedy Center, the National Storytelling Festival, and museums, schools, libraries, and festivals internationally.

His retelling of the story The Barking Mouse was published as a picture book in 2003. He released two additional picture books by Abrams Books for Young Readers in 2010. He is a frequent commentator on National Public Radio's *Latino USA*. His storytelling recordings have won numerous awards, including the American Library Association's Notable Recipient Award, the Parent's Choice Gold and Silver Awards, and the National Association of Parenting Publications Gold Award. He was also awarded an Ethnic and Folk Arts Fellowship from the Illinois Arts Council.

As a solo performer, Sacre has performed in festivals and theatres in New York City, Los Angeles, Minneapolis, San Francisco, and Chicago, where he performed under the tutelage and mentorship of Jenny Magnus at The New York City International Fringe Theatre Festival. Sacre was awarded a Best in Fringe Festival Award for Excellence in Acting, and a Best in Fringe Festival Award for Excellence in Solo Performance.

Since 1994, Antonio has taught drama, storytelling, and writing to teachers and students nationwide, and worked as artist in residence with youth in four inner city high schools of New York, Chicago, and South Central Los Angeles. He is a sought-after keynote speaker for diversity training across the country.

Ana Cristina Álvarez, known artistically as "Ana Cristina", is a singer who was born in Miami. She is known for her bluesy contralto vocals and rare "Whistle Register". Ana writes songs in the Pop/Soul genre with the help of the guitar and piano. She has worked with several Grammy award winning music producers throughout her career and was signed by Sony Music at the age of 15 where she first began recording in the Spanish language. Ana started her career by performing as a child on the long-running Univision variety show, "Sabado Gigante" from the age of 6 to 13.

At the age of 19, she became the first Hispanic woman in history to perform the "Star Spangled Banner" at a Presidential Inauguration in 2005 and won the title of Miss South Beach USA in 2011. Ana most notably gave a performance in 2006 at the White House in honor of Hispanic Heritage month serenading the President of the United States, the Crowned Prince of Spain and notable world ambassadors in the East Room with her potent voice. That same year, she recorded the theme song for the World

Cup Germany 2006 for the Univision Network titled "You Can Change the World" and its bilingual counterpart "El Mundo Puedes Cambiar".

Ana Cristina has also headlined the Calle Ocho Music Festival in Miami and has performed at NFL, MLB, NBA games, Madison Square Garden, The Sony Ericsson, as well as during both New York and Miami fashion week. She has been interviewed and performed multiple times on Univision and Telemundo network talk shows and has been featured in such publications as Cosmopolitan in Español, Glamour en Español, the cover of *The Miami Herald* to name a few. She is a prominent member of the Cuban-American/Latin community and in 2012, she was featured in Billboard En Español's "Hottest Latin Female Singers Under 30" list. (Preceding information taken from anacristina.com).

Jose Azel was born in Havana on August 18th, 1953. While earning a B.A. from Cornell University he began shooting pictures as a hobby. After completing his Master's in Journalism at the University of Missouri, he worked as a staff photographer at *The Miami Herald*. Teaming up with fellow photographer Bob Caputo, Azel founded a photojournalism group in 1993 called Aurora and Quanta Productions.

Dedicated to international, in-depth photojournalism, he specializes in broad geographic reporting. Adventure and an interest in environmental problems have led him to locations as diverse as the icy waters off Antarctica and Alaska to the game reserves of Kenya and the jungle of Borneo. His coverage of the 1984 and 1988 Summer Olympics earned him the prestigious World Press Photo

Foundation Amsterdam Olympic Award and the Marion Scubin Sport Award.

In 1988 he devoted the majority of his time to a 48 page article on cocaine for *National Geographic*. His work resulted in an invitation from Tufts University to serve as a guest lecturer at a major conference on drugs. He has also been a lecturer for the National Press Photographer Association Flying Short Course. Azel's photos have appeared regularly in *Smithsonian, Life, Connoisseur, The London Times* magazine, and Germany's *Geo*. He makes his home in Lovell, Maine. (Preceding information taken from photography.nationalgeographic.com).

Mike "In the Night" Triay was born and raised in Puerto Rico of Cuban parents. He came to Miami with his family in the late 1970s. Soon he began working as a disc jockey at a Spanish-language radio station in Miami while he was still in his late teens. He became well known as part of the production team responsible for the mid-'90s hit *Macarena* in the United States.

Mike Triay, Carlos de Yarza and radio personality Jammin Johnny Caride were the Bayside Boys, whose English-language remix of Spanish duo Los del Rio's song *Macarena* turned what had been a popular song in Latin America and U.S. Latin clubs into a major worldwide hit. The trio added English lyrics sung by Carla Vanessa and a dance beat better suited to U.S. audiences. The result, *Macarena (Bayside Boys Remix)*, topped Billboard's Hot 100 singles chart in 1996, and stayed there for 14 weeks, becoming one of the biggest radio hits in history. It's simple, catchy lyrics and distinctive dance made it a pop-culture and party mainstay. Triay, who also produced voiceovers and commercials, retired from commercial radio in 2010 but continued to run an Internet radio station, In the House radio. Tragically, Mike passed away on December 9th, 2012, after suffering a heart attack.

Midy Aponte is a first generation Cuban American and the President/CEO of The Sanchez Ricardo Agency, Washington, D.C. She is a graduate of Florida International University's School of Journalism and Mass Communications and resides in the nation's capital. As a bicultural communications strategist with more than 12 years in the industry, Midy is a sought-after expert in conceptualizing and executing multi-faceted campaigns, coalition-building efforts and media relations for non-profit organizations, businesses and government agencies. In 2009, she founded The Sanchez Ricardo Agency, a nonpartisan communications firm in Washington, D.C that provides expert counsel in the areas of digital media and multicultural public relations.

Prior to founding her company, Midy served as a Vice President at the Walker Marchant Group, a public affairs and issues management firm in Washington. There she represented Fortune 500 companies and multinational corporations, spearheading media relations and issues management strategies. Midy's background includes a strong history in social justice, advocacy and youth empowerment. While at GolinHarris, an international public relations firm and member of Interpublic Group, Midy designed social marketing movements and authored educational curriculum for nearly a dozen state health departments on grassroots methods to educate and mobilize teens to become activists for youth smoking prevention.

This included collaborating with the American Legacy Foundation, creators of a smoking cessation program, Become An Ex.

Midy frequently speaks before youth audiences, including the Girl Scouts' Encuentros de Chicas Latinas and College Bound, an academic mentoring program in the District of Columbia. She was nominated for an "Entrepreneurial Spirit Award" from the Women's Information Network (WIN) for their 2010 Women of Achievement Awards and was featured in *Hispanic Executive Magazine* as a "Mover and Shaker".(Preceding information taken from National Hispana Leadership Institute).

Marco Rizo Ayala (November 30, 1920- September 8, 1998) born in Santiago de Cuba, was a pianist, composer, and arranger. He is perhaps best known for his role as pianist, arranger and orchestrator for the American television sitcom *I Love Lucy* which aired from 1951 to 1957. He combined the techniques of classical training with Afro-Cuban and jazz rhythms, Rizo recorded nearly 30 albums.

In 1930 Rizo moved to Havana to attend the National Conservatory of Music; he remained there for six years, and in 1938 was named the official pianist of the Havana Philharmonic Orchestra, performing under the direction of musical icon Ernesto Lecuona. In 1940 he migrated to the United States having received a scholarship to the prestigious Juilliard School of Music in New York City. There, he studied under famed professor Rosina Lhevinne. Rizo performed and orchestrated with the 2nd Army Military Band during World War II. After the war, his childhood friend Desi Arnaz asked Rizo to join him as the pianist and orchestrator for his band, the Desi Arnaz Orchestra.

He toured the U.S. with the band until 1950; when Arnaz started production of *I Love Lucy*, he once again reached out to Rizo, hiring him to be the pianist and orchestrator for the show between 1951 and 1957.

Rizo also made several cameo appearances on the show throughout its run on television. He did not write the *I Love Lucy* theme by himself which had music by Rizo, Eliot Daniel and Desi Arnaz with lyrics by Harold Adamson. The lyrics were only heard once on the third season's episode "Lucy's Last Birthday" made in 1953. After the sitcom ended, he remained with CBS and was the pianist-arranger for the "Bob Hope Radio Show". While in Los Angeles, he attended UCLA and studied under Igor Stravinsky and Mario Castelnuovo-Tedasco.

Rizo composed motion picture music for Columbia, Paramount and MGM studios. He continued his concert career in 1960, playing the music of Lecuona and other Cubans. In the early 1970s, Rizo worked as the musical director for the Royal Viking Sea cruise ship. During his long career he arranged for hundreds of top artists such as Carmen Miranda, Danny Kaye, Xavier Cugat, Yma Sumac, and Paquito D'Rivera, among many others. In the early 1980s, he founded the non-profit organization "The Marco Rizo Latin American Music Project" which aimed to spread appreciation for Latin music and culture to students. Rizo won the Silver Medal of the French Academy of the Arts, Sciences and Letters for outstanding achievements in the field of Latin music. As cited in his web page, Rizo had a light, sure touch, and his playing combined classical technique with the syncopation of the Afro-Cuban tradition and the swing of jazz.

New York City native Ron Magill has more than three decades of service as a wildlife advocate for the Miami Metrozoo, now renamed Zoo Miami. He is the Communications Director and wildlife photographer as well. He rose to fame after Hurricane Andrew devastated the zoo in 1992; Magill was constantly on national TV, drawing the country's attention and millions of dollars in donations. The whole nation was touched by the plight of the animals. That's when he made a name for himself, and the zoo was reborn.

Magill has expanded the mission of the zoo and goes on many wildlife expeditions to places like the Serengeti Plains in Africa, diving with sea lions off the Galapagos Islands near South America, or studying eagles with his children in the rainforests of Panama. He has made regular appearances on "The Late Show with David Letterman", in Discovery Channel documentaries and other national programs. He is also a popular guest in Spanish-language TV hit show "Sabado Gigante", where the bilingual Magill delights the audience with his knowledge of wildlife. Years ago he handled all the animals used on the 1980s TV series "Miami Vice".

In 2006, Magill received the Wildlife Ambassador Award in recognition of his efforts on wildlife preservation. He has also been director for the Cheetah Conservation Program. Ron is an award-winning photographer and documentary producer whose images have appeared in publications and galleries around the world including the Smithsonian Museum of Natural History.

An obituary in *The Miami Herald* dated September 23, 2012 discusses the life and career of Jose Curbelo (1917-

2012), a Latin jazz band leader, agent and promoter who helped popularize the cha-cha-cha in the United States and made Tito Puente a star. Curbelo was born in Cuba to a Cuban mother and a Cuban-American father who studied violin in the United States and later played with the Havana Philharmonic Orchestra. Curbelo started his musical training at the age of 8. As a teen he played with Los Hermanos Le Batard and flutist-composer Gilberto Valdes and co-founded Orquesta Havana Riverside, in the 1930s, which still exists.

He eventually settled in New York in 1939 and formed a band that played Manhattan, the Catskill resorts, Miami, and Las Vegas. It was during this period that Puente got his start with Curbelo. The article mentions that Curbelo was one of the first ones educating American people on Latin and Cuban music. He was beloved by musicians and disliked by club owners because he would not book a gig unless it paid his asking price, according to his son Rene Curbelo. A piece in *The New York Times* notes that among his memorable recordings are a 1947 rendition of "Managua, Nicaragua" for RCA Victor and "Cha Cha Cha in Blue" and "La Familia" on Fiesta. How influential was Curbelo in the music scene? A 1978 article in *Latin New York* magazine said, "While most people identify the title 'King of Latin Music' with Tito Puente, few realize who is the power behind the throne...the person is Jose Curbelo".

Cuban-born Roymi V. Membiela is Corporate VP Marketing & Public Relations, Baptist Health South Florida, Coral Gables, Florida, the largest not-for-profit healthcare organization in its region. She is responsible for the strategic implementation of integrated marketing communications for the organization, internally and externally, as well as the immersion of the organization in digital marketing, leading all other healthcare organizations in South Florida in this field.

Roymi earned a Master of Science in Leadership from Nova Southeastern University in 2009, and a Bachelor of Professional Studies-Marketing degree from Barry University in 1986, and was inducted in the school's Alumni Hall of Fame in 1995. She holds an active State of Florida Real Estate License, and is accredited as a Certified County Court Mediator by the State of Florida Supreme Court.

Her career path includes more than 15 years of success as a senior executive of Knight Ridder's *The Miami Herald* and *El Nuevo Herald*, two national award-winning newspapers. While at the *Herald*, she was responsible for multiple advertising, marketing, and new business development initiatives. Roymi also managed the newspaper's business expansion to Latin America and the conceptualization of one of the nation's leading Spanish-language publications- *El Nuevo Herald*. She is the recipient of several awards including the 2010 Hispanic Women of Distinction Award and has received recognition from the U.S. Hispanic Chamber of Commerce as a Corporate Hispanic Business Advocate and by VISTA Magazine's 1997 VISTA Achievement Award for Hispanic Women.

Membiela serves on the Board of Directors of several community organizations, including the Health Foundation of South Florida; Community Habilitation Center; and the Miami-Dade County Hispanic Affairs Advisory Board. She is the past Chair of the City of Miami Beach's Community Relations Board, and past Vice Chair of the

Miami-Dade Expressway Authority. (Preceding information from National Hispana Leadership Institute).

Jose Manuel Carreño was born in Cuba and at the age of eight began studying ballet with Alicia Alonso, Lazaro Carreño (his uncle) and Loipa Araujo. He trained at the Provincial and National Ballet Schools in Cuba and immediately joined the National Ballet of Cuba.

Carreño won the prestigious Gold Medal in the New York International Ballet Competition (1987) and was later awarded the coveted Grand Prize at the USA International Competition in Jackson, Mississippi (1990), from which he accepted an invitation from Ivan Nagy to join English National Ballet as Principal Dancer.

In 1993, the Director of England's Royal Ballet, Sir Anthony Dowell, invited Carreño to become a principal dancer in The Royal Ballet. In 1995 Carreño was invited by American Ballet Theater's Artistic Director Kevin McKenzie to join ABT as Principal Dancer. He joined a year later, further expanding his repertory to include roles as diverse as Balanchine's *Apollo*, Danilo in The *Merry Widow*, Frank in *Coppelia*, Prince Siegfried in *Swan Lake*, Romeo in *Romeo and Juliet*, among other roles.

Carreño has danced with most of the great ballerinas of recent years, including Alicia Alonso, Carla Fracci, and Alessandra Ferri to name a few. Twyla Tharp and Nacho Duato regard him as an outstanding interpreter of their choreographies. Carreño is an acclaimed guest artist around the world, dancing in galas and with companies such as Bolshoi Ballet, Kirov Ballet, National Ballet of Canada, among others. He was nominated for a dance "Oscar" as one of the world's supreme male classical soloists of the new millennium (Monte Carlo 2000) and *Dance Magazine* awarded him Male Dancer of the Year in 2005. On June 30, 2011, he gave his final performance with the ABT in New York City at the Metropolitan Opera House in *Swan Lake* featuring Juliet Kent and Gillian Murphy as Odille and Odette. (Preceding information taken from jacobspillow.org).

Xavier Cortada, born in Albany, New York, is one of South Florida's most celebrated artists. He holds degrees from the University of Miami College of Arts and Sciences, Graduate School of Business and School of Law. He also serves as Artist-in-Residence and heads the Office of Engaged Creativity at Florida International University's College of Architecture + The Arts (CARTA). Cortada is also Artistic Director and Founder, the Reclamation Project, Miami Science Museum, Miami, Florida.

As noted on his web site, Cortada created art installations at the North Pole and South Pole to address environmental concerns at every point in between. He's been commissioned to create art for the White House, the World Bank, Miami City Hall, Miami-Dade County Hall, Florida Botanical Gardens, the Miami Art Museum, Museum of Florida History, Miami Science Museum and the Frost Museum. In addition, he has also developed numerous collaborative art projects globally, including peace murals in Cyprus and Northern Ireland, child welfare murals in Bolivia and Panama, AIDS murals in Geneva and South Africa, and eco-art projects in Taiwan, Holland, Hawaii and Latvia.

The artist is also a much sought-after speaker about his art. Cortada has delivered lectures at such prestigious institutions as Auburn University, Parsons The New School for Design, Princeton University, San Jose State University and the United States Embassy in Helsinki, Finland, among others. Part of his artist's statement includes the following, "My work aims to challenge us to find deeper meaning in our present lives by exploring the paths of those who came before us and our relationships to the natural world".

If one enjoys the sounds and rhythms of percussionists, then Luis Conte is the musician to listen to. His official website highlights a list of impressive accomplishments: "Percussionist of the Year"- Modern Drummer Reader's Poll (2009, 2010, 2011, 2012); "Percussionist of the Year"- Drum Magazine (2007, 2008, 2009) and "Studio Percussionist of the Year"- Drum Magazine (2007, 2008, 2009). Grammy-winner Luis Conte is truly an acknowledged master of percussion. His celebrated career includes touring and/ or recording work with some of the greatest names in contemporary music, including Madonna, Eric Clapton, Phil Collins, Santana, Jackson Browne, Celine Dion, Barbara Streisand, Ray Charles, Tony Bennett, James Taylor, Shakira, Ozzy Osborne, Queen Latifah, and Cuban legends Arturo Sandoval and Cachao.

Conte can also be heard on the scores and/or soundtracks to such box office hits as Transformers, Transformers 2, Hancock, Bruno, Superbad, the new Miami Vice, The Lost City with Andy Garcia, Mission Impossible, Rain Man, Waiting to Exhale, and countless others. Luis is also a percussionist for the orchestra on NBC's hit TV show, Dancing with the Stars.

Endorsed by the Meinl and Zildijian instrument companies, Luis has designed his own signature series of instruments and drumsticks. His percussion clinic tours take him around the world teaching musicians the essentials and history of Afro-Cuban rhythm. He also released his signature line of congas, timbales and shakers by Meinl, which were unveiled at NAMM 2005.

Can a young boy, raised on a remote farm in Cuba, and without any formal education in his chosen field, find fame and glory as a graphic designer and film title designer in New York? If you happen to be Pablo Ferro, the answer is a resounding yes. Born in 1935, Pablo moved with his parents to New York as a teenager and shortly thereafter taught himself animation from a book by Preston Blair. Then in the 1950s he began freelancing in the New York animation industry for Academy Picture and Elektra Studios. Later he met and befriended former Disney animator Bill Tytla, who became his mentor. Another co-worker was Stan Lee, the then-future editor of Marvel Comics, with whom he created a series of science fiction adventure comics. In 1961 Ferro became one of the partners to form Ferro, Mogubgub and Schwartz and in 1964 he founded Pablo Ferro Films.

A piece in *Art of the Title* tells that Pablo Ferro has been putting his stamp on the moving image through works such as the opening of Stanley Kubrick's "Dr. Strangelove" and the revolutionary split screen montage of 1963's "The Thomas Crown Affair". He has also created the opening titles for Hal Ashby's "Being There" (1979) and Gus Van Sant's "To Die For" (1995). An article from adcglobal.org credits Ferro with introducing the kinetic quick-cut method of editing whereby static images, including engravings, photographs, and pen and ink drawings, were infused with speed, motion, and sound. In addition, in the late 1950s he pioneered the use of type in motion on the TV screen, often using vintage wood types and Victorian gothics.

Pablo Ferro as writer Steve Heller reveals, for the title of "The Thomas Crown Affair", Ferro introduced multi-screen effects for the first time in any feature motion picture, defining a cinematic style of the late 1960s. Ferro acted as supervising editor for Michael Jackson's 1983 music video "Beat It", and co-directed with Hal Ashby the Rolling Stones' concert film "Let's Spend the Night Together", in which he introduced time-lapsed photography sequences. In 1992, he directed his own feature, "Me, Myself and I", starring George Segal and Jo Beth Williams.

The following are some of the awards from his distinguished career:

2009- AIGA Gold Award "in recognition for introducing narrative and nonlinear dimensions to design for films, changing our visual expectations and demonstrating the power of design to enhance storytelling"- AIGA

2002- Smithsonian Cooper-Hewitt, National Design Museum

2000- Art Directors Club- Hall of Fame

1999- Chrysler Design Award- Daimler-Chrysler

1961- 1965 Multiple CLIO Awards

1961- Formula 409- ADCO, Springfield

1962- U.S. Steele- BBDO, N.Y.

1963- Ford- J.W.T., N.Y. + Madame

1964- Huntley- Brinkley Report- NBC

1965- Beech Nut- Benton Bowles, N.Y.

Filmmaker Joe Menéndez was born in New York City of Cuban parents and raised in Miami. Joe was named one of *The Top 100 Latinos on the Move* by Latino Impact Magazine. Menendez's feature directing credits include his debut, *Lords of the Barrio*, which he also wrote and edited. His second feature, *Hunting of Man*, won Best Picture at the New York Latino International Film. In addition to his film work, Menendez has directed more than 57 hours of television, written numerous teleplays and produced a reality TV show.

Menendez began his filmmaking career at seven commandeering his grandmother's Super 8 movie camera to direct, shoot and edit movies starring his younger brother, cousins and friends. This early filmmaking continued including working as a cameraman and editor in the sports department of Univision's Miami affiliate at 17, while making short films at Miami-Dade Community College. A stint as a cameraman and editor followed at Miami's Jewish Federation Television, where he also directed various talk shows.

This hands-on experience provided the inspiration for the mostly self-taught filmmaker to move to Los Angeles at 22. Landing various odd-jobs including writing and producing on-air promos for Fox in Latin America, his break came at 24 when he was hired as a staff writer on a soap opera.

After, he quickly landed his first directing job on *Real Stories of the Highway Patrol*, where Menendez's slick-looking reenactments helped make the show a national syndicated success. From *Real Stories*, he moved to *Placas* for Telemundo. Over a three-year period, he directed 215 reenactments along with editing and often writing these mini movies.

His extensive television directing credits include winning an Alma Award for Outstanding Directing in a Comedy for Nickelodeon series *The Brothers Garcia* in 2001. As a writer, Menendez's other scripting credits include the PBS kids' show *Dragon Tales,* and staff writer on Fox's Luis Guzman sitcom, and HBO's *The Twelve Dancing Princesses.* Also a producer, he along with his wife, Roni Menendez, produced the reality television series *Urban Jungle* for SITV, under their company's Narrow Bridge banner. (Preceding information taken from www.filmbug.com).

Carmen Agra Deedy was born in Havana and came to the United States as young refugee in 1964. She was raised in Decatur, Georgia, where she lives today. She has been writing for children for over twenty years. Deedy began writing as a young mother and storyteller whose NPR commentaries on All Things Considered were collected and released under the title, Growing Up Cuban in Decatur, Georgia. The pithy collection of twelve stories soon garnered awards, among them a 1995 Publishers Weekly Best Audio (Adult Storytelling) and a 1996 Parents' Choice Gold Award.

Her children's books have won numerous awards. The Library Dragon received various children's state book awards and has sold nearly half a million copies. In 2003 the book was her home state's choice to represent Georgia at the Library of Congress's National Book Festival. The Yellow Star was the recipient of the 2001 Jane Addams Peace Association Book Award (Honor), presented to Ms. Deedy at the United Nations by Mrs. Kofi Annan. It also received the 2001 Christopher Award, the 2000 Parent's Choice Gold Award, the 2001 Bologna Ragazzi Award (for best international children's book), the 2002 WOW Award (National Literary Association of England), among other notable distinctions and honors. It has been translated to over a dozen languages.

Martina the Beautiful Cockroach was presented with the 2008 Pura Belpre Honor Award, the 2008 NCSS/CBC Notable Social Studies Book Award, the 2008 Best Children's Books of the Year (Bank Street College of Education), the 2008 International Latino Book Award, the Irma Simonton and James H. Black Award (Honor), the 2008 E.B. White Award (Nominee), and the 2009 ALA Odyssey Audio Award (Honor), among others.

Ms. Deedy's most recent children's book, 14 Cows for America, is based on an astonishing gift Americans received from a Maasai village in Kenya, following the events of 9/11. The book was released in September of 2009 and is a *New York Times* Bestseller. *The Wall Street Journal* described it as a "...moving and dramatically illustrated picture book." Carmen is now expanding into the world of chapter books with her Fall 2011 title, The Cheshire Cheese Cat: A Dickens of a Tale. This is a story of deception, intrigue, and derring-do that reveals the unlikely alliance between a cheese-loving cat and the Cheshire Cheese Inn mice in Victorian England.

She has been an invited speaker at venues as varied as The American Library Association, Refugees International, The International Reading Association, Columbia University, The Smithsonian Institute, TED, The National Book Festival, and the Kennedy Center. An ardent supporter of libraries, she was the 2008 National Spokesperson for School Library Media Month (AASL). She has spoken before Noble Laureates and Pulitzer Prize winners, CEOs of major corporations, and heads of states. But children still remain her favorite audience. (The above information is from Carmen's web page).

Actress Olga Merediz was born in Cuba and raised in Puerto Rico. She is a Broadway, TV, and film actress. Merediz is probably best known for originating the role of Claudia in the Broadway musical In the Heights, where she received a Tony Award nomination. She played the role for the show's entire Broadway run. Some of her other Broadway credits include Reckless, Man of La Mancha, and Les Miserables. She also appeared as Rosie in Mamma Mia!. Merediz has appeared off-Broadway in Women Without Men, The Human Comedy, and The Public Theater's NYSF The Taming of the Shrew in Central Park.

She has also appeared in TV shows, including Pan Am, Blue Bloods, Royal Pains, Law & Order, The Jury, Hope & Faith, and George Lopez. She appeared in the film Remember Me as a professor. Olga appeared with Jim Carrey in Mr. Popper's Penguins, John Leguizamo in Fugly, Meryl Streep in Music of the Heart, Madonna in Evita, Kevin Spacey in K-Pax, and Samuel L. Jackson in Changing Lanes.

She was a 2007 Drama Desk Award for Outstanding Ensemble Performance for her work in the off-Broadway run of In the Heights, as well as a 2007 HOLA Award from the Hispanic Organization of Latin Actors for Outstanding Performance by a Featured Female Actor. At the 2008 Tony Awards, she received a nomination for Best Perfor-

67

mance by a Featured Actress in a Musical for the Broadway incarnation of In the Heights.

Coco Fusco was born in New York City on June 18, 1960 to Cuban parents who had emigrated in 1954. Shortly after the 1959 Cuban Revolution, her father was deported. Her mother hid from the INS and did not return to Cuba until after Coco was born. As her relatives immigrated to New York, throughout the 1960s, Coco's home served as a gateway to life in the U.S. Fusco was raised in this bicultural setting, where the private and public spheres of daily life was thrown into sharp relief because of differences in language, culture, and tradition.

Coco attended Brown University where she obtained a B.A. in Literature and Society; then achieved a M.A. in Modern Thought and Literature from Stanford University, and finally a doctorate in Visual Culture from Middlesex University in England. She began her career as an assistant professor of Visual Arts at Temple University; she became an associate professor in 1988, holding the position until 2001, when she transferred to be an associate professor at the School of the Arts at Columbia University in New York City.

She is an interdisciplinary artist, writer, and curator. Her videos, performances, and art installations have been showcased throughout the world to great critical acclaim, and her published writing on art, culture, and politics have helped shape the field of Latina and Latino studies, performance studies, and postcolonial studies. She is a public writer, and cultural commentator as well as an innovative artist whose work blurs the boundaries between cultural theory and artistic practice.

Fusco was the recipient of the 1995 ATHE Research Award for Outstanding Journal Article and the 1995 Critics' Choice Award for her book, *English is Not Broken Here*. She has also participated in eleven different curatorial projects and in many lectures and conferences at universities and art schools since 1987. In 2012, Fusco was named a Fellow of United States Artists. (Preceding information taken from 2017blackart.wordpress.com).

Emilio Cruz (1938-2004) was born in New York City where he lived most of his life. An African-American of Cuban origin, his continued deliberation on the mythic dimensions of human experience and expression carried through his multiple identities and activities as a virtual artist, poet, playwright and musician. For many years this veteran artist worked on paintings that involved large themes alluding to archetypes from a trans-cultural web of belief systems and traditions.

Cruz was convinced that in order to produce art of significance, one must have a clear commitment to humanity and its universal moral imperatives. He said, integrity is formulated by acknowledging those things that we find inform us about the nature of the human spirit. The word inspired means 'in the spirit' (Being) in the spirit is always avant garde. For this reason Paleolithic art always seems new, because it defines the moment of inspiration, through the certainty of "truth".

He exhibited nationally and internationally and is represented in numerous museum collections, including the Museum of Modern Art, the Brooklyn Museum, the Studio Museum in Harlem, New York; the National Museum of American Art and the Hirschhorn Museum of Art,

Washington, D.C.; the Albright Knox Museum, Buffalo, New York; and the Wadsworth Athenaeum, Hartford, Connecticut. The artist received many honors, including a John Jay Whitney Fellowship and awards from the National Endowment for the Arts and the Joan Mitchell Foundation.

Harry Rand, Curator of 20th Century Painting and Sculpture at the Smithsonian American Art Museum, described Emilio Cruz as one of the important pioneers of American Modernism of the 1960s, for his fusion of abstract expressionism with figuration. Cruz studied at the Art Students League and The New School in New York, then at the University of Louisville in Kentucky, and finally at the Seong Moy School of Painting and Graphic Arts in Provincetown, Massachusetts. ( Preceding information taken in part from emiliocruz.com).

Songwriter and producer Desmond Child is one of modern music's most successful creative forces. He was born in 1953 in Gainesville, Florida and was raised in Miami and Ponce, Puerto Rico where his Cuban songwriter mother, Elena Casals, taught him to play the piano at an early age. His mother was the composer of "Muchisimo", "Noches de Maracaibo", "Ponce" and "Diosa del Mar". She was also the sister-in-law of famed Cuban singer Olga Guillot. In Miami he studied at Miami-Dade College and formed the group Desmond Child and Rouge in 1973. The band moved to New York City and recorded two albums and had a dance hit, "Our Love Is Insane" which reached #50 on the Billboard Hot 100 in 1979.

Child's experience as a recording artist would soon play a role in his songwriting career. His songs caught the attention of KISS guitarist Paul Stanley and Child wrote "I Was Made for Loving You", which is still one of the biggest hits in the KISS catalogue. He also collaborated in writing Bon Jovi's first number-one-single, "You Give Love a Bad Name". From then on he started working with other major recording artists like Aerosmith, Joan Jett, Alice Cooper, Michael Bolton and Cher.

In 1993, Desmond wrote a song in Spanish titled "Tu Seras la Historia de Mi Vida", for Colombian singer Shakira's second studio album, *Peligro*. In the late 1990s, Child returned to his Latin heritage by collaborating with Ricky Martin. Their efforts resulted in the number-one- worldwide smash "Livin' La Vida Loca". The two also worked on "The Cup of Life", which was used as the official song of the 1998 FIFA World Cup. The single reached the top of the charts in 25 countries. Child is a member of the Songwriters Hall of Fame. His list of accomplishments include Grammy awards, 70 Top 40 singles, and songs that have sold over 300 million albums worldwide.

Director, producer, music video director Brett Ratner was born in Miami Beach in 1969. His mother was originally from Cuba, born to Eastern European Jews who had immigrated to the island nation. Ratner was raised by his mother and grandparents and considers himself Jewish and Cuban. Although he is not fluent in Spanish, he loves to eat traditional Cuban food such as *picadillo, boliche,* and *pollo asado*. But he says he always starts with *croquetas* and washes it down with a *mamey* milkshake. Brett makes it a habit whenever he flies to Miami to stop off at the iconic Versailles Restaurant in Little Havana to enjoy typical Cuban fare.

Ratner graduated from high school in Miami Beach and then continued his education by earning a degree from the Film School at New York University in 1990. He received a scholarship from Steven Speilberg's production company in his senior year to fund his thesis project, a documentary about former child star Mason Reese. He started his professional career directing music videos for such artists as P. Diddy, Mariah Carey, Mary J. Blige and Jay-Z.

He has been a very busy and successful director and producer. The following are some of Ratner's film and television work since 1997:

*Money Talks*- Director
*Rush Hour*- Director
*Family Man*- Director
*Rush Hour 2*- Director
*Red Dragon*- Director
*After the Sunset*- Director
*Prison Break* (Pilot episode)- Director
*X-Men: The Last Stand*- Director
*2006 Becker Hargrove, Inc.* (Short film)- Producer
*Rush Hour 3*- Director
*21*- Producer
*New York, I Love You*- Director
*Kites: The Remix*- Director
*Skyline*- Producer
*Tower Heist*- Director
*Horrible Bosses*- Producer
*2011Mother's Day*- Producer
*Mirror Mirror*- Producer

*Movie 43-* Director

*Hercules: The Thracian Way-* Director


René Echevarría is a Cuban-American writer, producer and story editor of many *Star Trek: The Next Generation* and *Star Trek: Deep Space Nine* episodes. He also appeared as a holographic bar patron in the final episode of *Deep Space Nine,* "What You Leave Behind".

After graduating with a degree in History from Duke University, Echevarria moved to New York to pursue a career in theater. In 1985, he was assistant director to a production of the Victor Muñiz play "Darts" and appeared in a production of "The Lower Depths" by Gorky. In 1986, he started in a production of the Kristin McCloy play "Isosceles" at the Chelsea Theater, and in 1987, he appeared in the La Mama Theater adaptation of the Aeschuylus play "Prepared", which was presented at the World's End Theater in London in 1988 and was performed at the Edinburgh Festival that same year.

In 1989, while working as a waiter in New York, he wrote his first script for *Star Trek: The Next Generation,* "The Offspring".

As a result, he became a regular writer for the show and was also a regular writer for *Star Trek: Deep Space Nine.* His 30-plus episodes of *Star Trek* have earned him a Humanitas nomination, a Peabody nomination, two Hugo nominations, and a NASA Vision award for Best Depiction of Humanity's Future in Space. In 1994, he received a Special Achievement award from the Latino Media organization HAMAS. In 1998, he developed the scenario for *Star Trek: The Experience.*

After *Star Trek* he was supervising producer on the critically acclaimed, but short-lived CBS series *Now and Again* distributed by Paramount Pictures. In 2000, he signed on as co-executive producer for the short-lived James Cameron FOX series *Dark Angel* as part of an overall multiyear deal with 20th Century FOX Television to develop new products for the studio.

On February 2013, Echevarria joined CBS' drama pilot *Intelligence* as executive producer/showrunner. He will be partnering with creator/executive producer Michael Seitzman in running the series for ABC Studios and CBS TV Studios. Echevarria served as executive producer/showrunner on FOX's *Terra Nova*. He also co-created USA's *The 4400* and worked on *Medium and Castle*. (Preceding information taken from en.memory-alpha.org, www.deadline.com).

Ozzie Alfonso is a well-known Award winning TV producer/writer/director and college professor. He was born in Cuba in 1945 and arrived in the United States at age 10. He lives in New York with his wife, a teacher and children's book author, Maura Gouck, and son, David.

Alfonso was the director and one of three senior producers of 3-2-1 Contact from season 2 to 8 when the series stopped production. He was also one of the writers for the series from season 3 through 8. Following production of the daily series, he was the director of all the 3-2-1 Contact Specials, and 3-2-1 Classroom. His work at 3-2-1 Contact garnered two Emmy Awards- for cinematography (contributing cinematographer), and for Outstanding Directing.

Prior to joining 3-2-1 Contact, Alfonso was a contributing director for Sesame Street where he started in the series second season as Post Production Supervisor and video editor. He was nominated for a nighttime Emmy for his directing in "Sesame Street in Puerto Rico". Alfonso's other Sesame credits include serving as associate director on the specials Christmas Eve on Sesame Street and Big Bird in China and directing celebrity segments on Shalom Sesame, such as those featuring Joan Rivers and Alan King.

He left Sesame Street in 1979 and returned to the Children's Television Workshop (now known as Sesame Workshop) to work in 3-2-1 Contact. After leaving Sesame Workshop, he freelanced as director and writer of numerous specials for PBS, Nickelodeon, and NBC. From 1991 to 2008, Alfonso headed his own video production and consulting company, Terra Associates, now Ozzie Alfonso Media, and is currently a professor at St. John's University in Queens, New York where he teaches general courses on media, television production, and writing. Alfonso is still an active director/writer working on selected projects.

Rudy Pérez is a musician, composer, producer, arranger, singer, entrepreneur and philanthropist who arrived in Miami at age 7 in 1965. He began his career at age 15 when he joined Pearly Queen, a Top 40 cover band that was popular in Miami in 1973. At age 20 he left the group to produce and write songs for local Latin singers in the South Florida area. During the last 30 years, Perez has produced more than 70 albums, composed over 1,000 songs, and has written and produced music for popular international stars. He also owns the record label, Rudy Perez Enterprises (RPE), and Bullseye Productions, and is a founding partner and the Chief Creative Officer in DIGA Entertainment. He was instrumental in the production of the premier of the inaugural Latin Grammy Awards in

2000. He was also one of the founders of the American Society of Composers, Authors and Publishers' (ASCAP) Latin Council.

His major breakthrough came in 1986 with the song "Ya Soy Tuyo" recorded by Jose Feliciano which earned Perez a Grammy Award for Producer of "Best Latin Pop Performance" and in 1988 he was elected "Producer of the Year". In 1993, he won another Grammy Award for Producer, and Songwriter for the "Best Latin Pop Album " (Aries), by Luis Miguel. In 1997 he wrote and produced the album "Lo Mejor De Mi"for Mexican singer Christian Castro whose hit "Lo Mejor De Mi" remained for more than 90 weeks on the charts. "Despues De Ti..Que?"(dedicated to Rudy's mother who died of cancer), and "Si Tu Me Amaras" were also major hits from the recording. The album reached #1 on Hot Latin Tracks of 1997 and it also received a nomination for Grammy Award for Best Latin Pop Album of 1998.

His compositions have reached numerous top ten hits the last 20 years, over 300 have been #1 or in the Top Ten hit parade. He also won the Hot Latin Songs, a record chart published by Billboard magazine, making him the first Hispanic composer and producer to win this award. The songs he composed and produced also earned him 30 Gold and 50 Platinum records. Perez has been classified as the most important Latin composer and won the title of Producer of the Decade in 2010, awarded by Billboard.

In 2003, Perez launched a scholarship program of the ASCAP Foundation (Rudy Perez Songwriting), which provides educational opportunities for talented Hispanics with limited resources to study at prestigious music schools worldwide. He donated $25,000 dollars to fund the first scholarship. The scholarships will rotate annually among students from different universities. The first scholarship is awarded in Miami, and the others are given to the Julliard School of Music in New York City, the National Conservatory of Music in Puerto Rico, and High School of Art and Music at The University of Texas at San Antonio.

Cecilia Sanmartín is an author, practicing psychotherapist and social worker with individuals and families from Mexico, Central and South America for more than 20 years. She studied Psychology at UCLA and Marriage and Family Therapy at Santa Clara University. Cecilia was born in Havana and raised in California; her parents where hard-working refugees who worked long hours and she was raised by her grandparents enabling her to be fluent in Spanish.

She has penned *Broken Paradise, Tarnished Beauty, Vigil, Mofongo* and her latest literary work, *Doña Maria.* Her books have been translated into Spanish, French, Dutch, German and Norwegian. Cecilia completed a successful book tour of Norway in 2009; she topped the best seller list there for over two years. Her books have also been released in Portugal, Finland and Italy. She lives with her family in the San Gabriel Valley, near Los Angeles.

Yalil Guerra was the Latin Grammy Winner 2012 for Best Classical Contemporary Composition "Seduccion". Yalil was born in Havana in 1973 and his first musical studies were at the National School of Music in Havana (1985-1991) with classical guitar professor and concert master Jorge Luis Zamora. At the age of 16 Guerra won the International Competition and Festival of Classical Guitar in Krakow, Poland, as well as the Special Prize (1990). He became the youngest Cuban awarded a prize in an international competition. He graduated as a classical guitar performer and professor in 1991.

He moved to Spain and obtained his Master's degree in Classical Guitar at the Royal Conservatory of Music "Queen Sofia" in Madrid. He also received composition classes with composer and professor Aurelio de la Vega, Emeritus professor at California State University, Northridge. He started his career as a producer, composer and arranger in 1990 and has worked with many companies and professionals. Some of the artists include Cristian Castro, Celia Cruz, Albita Rodriguez, Eddie Santiago, Rey Ruiz and Yamila Guerra to name a few.

Yalil now writes music for U.S. TV networks such as Univision, Tele Futura; the music of shows such as FIFA World Cup music theme 2010, "Viva el Sueño" (2009), the Latin Grammy Awards (2005-2011), "Premio lo Nuestro" (2006-2011), Up Front (2005 and 2006), "Escandalo TV", "Tributo a Nuestra Musica"; "Premios Juventud"; "Sabado Gigante"; "Mira Quien Baila"; are among his credits. Yalil composes and produces albums at his recording studio in Burbank, California. In 2010, Guerra was awarded Runner-Up by the Brandon Fradd Fellowship in Music Composition sponsored by the Cintas Foundation and the Frost Art Museum of Florida International University 2010.

Four awarded compositions have been included in his album entitled "Old Havana. Chamber Music Vol. I" nominated by the Latin Recording Academy in the Best

Classical album category 2010. In 2011 he released his second album titled "Old Havana. Chamber Music Vol. II". ( Information for this article taken from the artist's web page).

Miami native Josie Loren is an actress best known for her role as Kaylie Cruz on the television drama series *Make It or Break It*. Josie began her television career by playing the character Holly on *Hannah Montana*, working with teen sensation Miley Cyrus in the episode "People Who Use People". She then took on a role in *Medium* and later appeared on two episodes of the Nickelodeon series *Drake & Josh* as Maria. In 2007, Loren was cast in the Disney series *Cory in the House*, playing the character Jessica on the episode "Get Smarter".

Loren also worked on *The Bill Engvall Show*, which led her to be chosen for a role in the short comedy *Hardly Married*. Loren followed it up with *Christmas in Paradise*, and then in 2008's comic drama, *This Is Not a Test*. She obtained further popularity with a role in the hit film, *17 Again*. In 2009, she was cast in the Disney television movie *Hatching Pete*. Later that year she appeared in a starring role on the ABC Family series *Make It or Break It*, a program which follows the adventures of a group of gymnasts hoping to make it to the Olympics. In 2001 she played Jayden in the short film *With Me* and in 2013 she plays Pledge Aguilar in *21 & Over*.

Luis P. Senarens (1865-1939) was born in Brooklyn, New York of Cuban parents. He was a prolific boys' fiction writer who began writing at the age of 12. At 14, he established an association with publisher Frank Tousey's periodical *Boys of New York* by writing the first of hundreds of adventures about Frank Reade, Jr., a teen-aged inventor extraordinaire. Tales such as *Frank Reade, Jr. and His Steam Wonder* (dealing with a steam locomotive and caboose constructed to run on roads and over plains instead of on tracks) and *Frank Reade, Jr., and His Electric Boat*, flowed from the boy's pen under the guise of Noname. The precocious Senarens did not reveal his actual age to his publisher for two years.

So popular were Reade's stories that the character was given his own weekly title in 1892 (also written by Senarens under the Noname pseudonym) named the Frank Reade Library. Over the course of 191 issues readers learned about a remarkable array of robots, air craft, submersibles, armored vehicles, and powered land and sea vessels. For more than thirty years, Senarens wrote some 40 million words and 1,500 individual stories under 27 pseudonyms, rarely leaving his home in Brooklyn. His prophetic output was so enormous that he earned the nickname the American Jules Verne. Some speculate that Verne himself, in fact, borrowed from Senarens the basic idea of grand steam-powered inventions for his own The Steam House (1880) and acknowledged it in a letter to the 14 year old (who was too embarrassed to reply immediately for fear his age might be discerned from his handwriting). (Information for this article taken from steampunk.wiki.com).

Jackie Nespral, a television anchor for WTVJ-TV, the NBC owned and operated station in South Florida, was born in Miami and raised in the Little Havana neighborhood. She began her entertainment and television career as a college student at the University of Miami, where she was elected Orange Bowl Queen in Miami in 1985 and

1986. Jackie graduated from the University of Miami with a B.A. degree in Psychology with a minor in Communications. She also completed two years of post-graduate studies in print and broadcast journalism at Florida International University.

Nespral began her career in television as spokes model for *Sabado Gigante* on Univision. She then joined Univision's *TV Mujer* on its final season. After the cancellation of that show, she was chosen as one of the anchors, in 1990, of Univision's national news show, *Noticias y Mas* ("News and More"). Jackie moved to New York City in 1991, where she became the first Hispanic American network television news anchor as the weekend co-host of NBC's *Today* with Scott Simon. In 1994, she returned to Miami, where she was assigned as anchorwoman for WTVJ-TV.

The distinguished journalist is a board director for the March of Dimes organization and the University of Miami. She is also involved with the Columbia Women's Center, South Miami Hospital's Child Development Center and the Amigos for Kids organizations. Jackie has earned four Emmy Awards, an Easter Seals award and an honorable mention from the American Women in Radio and Television organization during her television news career. She has also received the key to the city of Miami and a Resolution of Tribute from the University of Miami. Nespral also was awarded with the highest honor achieved at the University of Miami, the Iron Arrow. (Preceding information from nbc.com).

Hector Samuel Juan 'Tico" Torres is a drums and percussionist for rock band Bon Jovi. He also has taken lead vocals on a song on the box set *100, 000,000 Bon Jovi Fans Can't Be Wrong*, as well as backing vocals on a couple of the early Bon Jovi tracks, notably "Born to Be My Baby" and "Love for Sale". Tico Torres was born on October 7th, 1953, in New York City; his parents emigrated from Cuba in 1948.

Torres was a jazz fan in his youth and in 1969 he played drums for the psychedelic rock band Six Feet Under and in the studio with Pat Benatar, Chuck Berry, Cher, Alice Copper, Stevie Nicks and others, recording a total of 26 albums with these artists. In 1983 Tico met Alec John Such while playing with a band and it was this friendship which led him to join Bon Jovi. Known as "The Hitman", Tico discovered another talent: painting. He has exhibited his art since 1994. The successful first show was at The Ambassador Galleries in Soho, New York. Tico is a self-taught painter, he paints expressive pictures which show scenes from everyday life and the life with the band. He also owns a fashion line for babies called Rock Star Baby, selling baby clothing, strollers, soft toys, jewelry and furniture.

Havana native Horacio "El Negro" Hernández is a renowned drummer and percussionist. "El Negro" first gained international recognition as the drummer for pianist Gonzalo Rubalcaba and his group Proyecto. Since leaving Cuba in 1990, Hernandez has made a name for himself in the United States with his live performances with many different pop, rock, jazz and Latin jazz acts and his appearances on many different albums, some of which have received Grammy awards, like Roy Hargrove's "Havana" (1997), Carlos Santana's "Supernatural" (1999), Alejandro Sanz's "No es lo mismo" (2003), and Eddie Palmieri's "Listen here", (2005).

Hernandez won a Grammy award for the 2001 Latin jazz album "Live at the Blue Note", with Michael Camino (piano) and Charles Flores (bass). Since 2004 he records and tours with his own band, Italuba. In 2011 he played at the Modern Drummer Festival with his new band The New World Order. Horacio is a member of the faculties of Drummer's Collective and the New School in New York, and regularly conducts clinics and workshops at the prestigious Berklee College of Music, as well for Pearl drums and Zidjian cymbals.

Pedro de Córdova (1881- 1950) was born in New York City to parents of French and Cuban origin. He was a classically trained actor who confessed he did not enjoy appearing in silent films nearly as much as he liked working on stage, but his career during the silent film era was extensive. His first film was Cecil B. DeMille's version of *Carmen* (1915), and he soon became a popular leading man in Hollywood. His Broadway career cast him with such stage actresses as Jane Cowl and Katherine Cornell.

Later in his career his deeply resonant speaking voice made him perfectly suited to talking pictures, and his film career continued, unlike many silent film stars. He enjoyed a career as a busy character actor in Hollywood, from the 1930s through to the end of his life. He was most often cast as an aristocratic, or clerical character of Hispanic origin, as in *The Keys of the Kingdom* (1944), because of his last name as well as royal bearing. On rare occasions, he would be cast in the role of villain. His "living skeleton" sideshow character hides fugitive Robert Cummings (and

Priscilla Lane) in his carnival wagon overnight in the Alfred Hitchcock movie *Saboteur* (1942).

He was a devout Catholic and was very well read and knowledgeable about the Catholic faith, and served for a time as president of the Catholic Actors Guild of America. The last film in which he appeared, a political drama set in an unnamed South American dictatorship, *Crisis* (1950), was released shortly after his death.

Born in Matanzas, Cuba, Silvia Curbelo emigrated to the U.S. with her family when she was a child. Her poetry has been published in literary journals and over two dozen anthologies such as The Body Electric; America's Best Poetry (W.W. Norton), Snakebird: Thirty Years of Anhinga Poets (Anhinga Press), and Norton's Anthology of Latino Literature.

She has received the Individual Artist Fellowship from the Florida Division of Cultural Affairs for poetry three times. In addition Curbelo has been awarded fellowships from the National Endowment for the Arts, the Seaside Institute, the Writer's Voice, the Florida Arts Council and Cintas Foundation for her poetry. She won the Atlantic Center for the Arts Cultural Exchange Fellowship to La Napoule Arts Foundation in France. In 1996, Curbelo won the Jessica Nobel-Maxwell Memorial Prize from the American Poetry Review.

Silvia Curbelo is published in the American Poetry Review, Kenyon Review, Gettysburg Review, Praire Schooney and Tampa Review in addition to others. She has authored three collections, The Geography of Leaving (Silverfish Review Press), The Secret History of Water (Anhinga Press) and Ambush (www.mainstreetag.com).

The Secret History of Water was the inaugural volume of the Anhinga Press Van K. Brock Florida Poetry Series. The most recent collection, Ambush, won the Main Street Rag Chapbook Competition. Curbelo currently lives and works in Tampa as an editor for Organica Quarterly. (Preceding information taken from tampagov.net).

Manny Coto was born of Cuban origin in Orlando, Florida. He is a writer, director and producer of films and television programs. He was the executive producer and showrunner of *Star Trek: Enterprise* in its final season. He is the co-executive producer on the fifth and sixth seasons of *24*.

Coto graduated from the American Film Institute and has had much experience in sci-fi and fantasy genre. He wrote and directed an episode of *Tales from the Crypt* and also wrote an episode for and produced *The Outer Limits* when it was revived on Showtime in 1995. He was given the chance to create and write a series for Showtime after *The Outer Limits* was cancelled. The resulting series was *Odyssey 5* and starred Peter Weller, the original *RoboCop* (Coto would later cast Weller in roles on both *Enterprise* and *24*).

He joined the writing crew of *Enterprise* in 2003, when the show was in its third season, and became a co-executive producer later that season. In the fourth season he became an executive producer of the show, alongside creators Rick Berman and Brannon Braga. He wrote a number of episodes of the series, such as *Similitude, Chosen Realm,* and *Azati Prime.*

According to his bio on StarTrek.com, he has been a fan of *Star Trek* all his life and once wrote a *Star Trek* comic book. Because of this, and his radical approach to tie in *Enterprise* with the original *Star Trek* and preserve continuity, it resulted in high support for his work from the fan base and he was largely credited with improving the quality of the series in its last season. Coto has also directed a number of films including *Dr. Giggles* and *Star Kid*. He is also a cast member on FOX News Channel's *The Half Hour News Hour*. (Preceding information taken from www.filmbug.com).

Cuban-American Jorge Moreno delivered some of the most interesting and alternative work to the Latin music scene in the early 2000s; a fusion of pop/rock, Afro-Cuban, Caribbean, and urban rhythms are brought together in his debut album, Moreno. Influenced by his father, Tony Moreno, a Latin music expert, and mother, who used to listen to American rock & roll and British pop, Jorge became involved in popular music while participating with a trio which disbanded after three years of playing internationally.

EMI Music Publishing gave him the opportunity to work as a songwriter, and Moreno later signed with the Latin division of Maverick. There he made his first solo album, produced by Andres Levin, A.T. Molina, and Lester Mendez. In addition, Moreno performed a memorable version of Desi Arnaz's "Babalu" in a special program to celebrate the 50th anniversary of the *I Love Lucy* show.

In 2002, Moreno won the 2002 Latin Grammy Award for Best New Artist, and in 2003 his album Moreno received a Grammy nomination for Best Latin Pop album. Interestingly, Moreno has often used the word "alternative" to categorize his music. Most recently, he is taking music at his own pace and is releasing a string of singles. The first being "Thank You" released late 2010 from Forward Motion Records on iTunes that won the prestigious International Songwriter Contest "ISC" award for "Best Video" and placed as a semi finalist for "Best Song". His second single "This Town" is an Orbison-esc indie track and was recently released on iTunes. (Preceding information taken from allmusic.com).

The De Castro Sisters were the Cuban version of the famous American singing group the Andrew Sisters. The De Castro siblings were Peggy, Bobette, and Cherie who were born in 1921, 1927 and 1925, respectively. They formed a close-harmony vocal trio who began their career in Cuba around 1940.

Their mother was an original Ziegfeld Follies girl and their father owned sugar plantations in the Dominican Republic and Cuba. After a successful nightclub act in Havana, the De Castro Sisters moved to Miami in 1945 and they were taken under the wing by Carmen Miranda, a Portuguese-born Brazilian samba singer, dancer, and film star of the 1940s and 1950s, appearing in her movie, Copacabana.

Signed to the small Abbott label, they had a smash hit in 1954 with "Teach Me Tonight", written by Sammy Cahn and Gene De Paul, which sold over 5 million copies. In 1955, they made the U.S. charts again, with "Boom Boom Boomerang". Other important 50s titles included "Too Late Now', "Snowbound for Christmas", It's Yours", "Who Are They To Say", "Cuckoo In The Clock", "Give Me Time" and "Cowboys Don't Cry".

Bobette retired in 1958 and was replaced in the group by their cousin Olguita De Castro. In 1959, they re-recorded their original hit as "Teach Me Tonight Cha Cha", perhaps a sign that their appeal, at least on records, was fading. Despite the rapidly changing musical climate, they released "Sing and Rockin' Beat" in the early 60s. More than 25 years later, in 1988, the De Castro Sisters hit the comeback trail at Vegas World, Las Vegas. Reliving 50s songs while also strutting to later anthems such as "New York, New York", they made up for tired vocal chords with an abundance of showbiz flair. Cherie De Castro, the last surviving member, passed away at age 87 on March 14th, 2010. (Preceding information taken from www.oldies.com).

Francisco Aguabella (1925-2010) was an Afro-Cuban percussionist of the Santeria religion who left Cuba in the 1950s and performed with Dizzy Gillespie, Tito Puente, Peggy Lee, Frank Sinatra, Eddie Palmieri, Carlos Santana and the Doors. Aguabella was considered a master sacred drummer who also had a wide-ranging career in jazz and salsa.

Aguabella was born in Matanzas, Cuba and at age 12 started playing the *bata*, a sacred drum shaped like an hourglass. He moved to Havana in 1947 and eventually started performing at one of the city's leading nightclubs, playing every form of Afro-Cuban drums. That's where dancer and choreographer Katherine Dunham saw him. He went with her dance troupe to Italy for the filming of "Mambo" and toured extensively with the group eventually making his way to the United States.

"Almost all the people who learned to play sacred drums had him as their teacher. He provided great continuity," said Raul Fernandez, author of *From Afro-Cuban Rhythms to Latin Jazz* and a professor in UC Irvine's Chicano/Latino studies program. "He was the carrier of the tradition....He was the only person in the United States who learned from Cuban masters." In 1992, Aguabella received a national heritage fellowship from the National Endowment for the Arts. He also taught at UCLA. Aguabella was featured in the documentary "Sworn to the Drum", released in 1995. "He was incredible, a wonderful musician and a great spirit", filmmaker Les Blank said. "I think he felt honored that we paid him the attention and respect that he deserved." Aguabella died at his home in Los Angeles at age 84. (Preceding information from articles.latimes.com/2010/may/09.).

Manuel Barrueco is internationally recognized as one of the most important guitarists of our time. He began playing the guitar at the age of eight, and he attended the Esteban Salas Conservatory in Cuba. He came with his family to the United States in 1967, as political refugees. Later, he completed his advanced studies at the Peabody Conservatory of Music, where he now shares his love for music with a small number of exceptionally gifted young guitarists from all over the world.

His career has been dedicated to bringing the guitar to the main musical centers of the world. During three decades of concertizing, he has performed across the United States from the New World Symphony in Miami to the Seattle Symphony, and from the Hollywood Bowl to New York's Lincoln Center. He has appeared with such prestigious orchestras as the Philadelphia Orchestra and with the Boston Symphony under the direction of Seiji Ozawa, in the American premiere of Toru Takemitsu's To the Edge of Dream.

His international tours include the Royal Albert Hall in London, Musikuverein in Vienna, Concertgebouw in Amsterdam, Philharmonie in Berlin, Teatro Real in Madrid, and Palau de la Musica in Barcelona. In Asia he has completed close to a dozen tours of Japan, and made repeated appearances in Korea, Taiwan, Singapore, and Hong Kong. Barrueco's tours of Latin America have included performances in Mexico, Brazil, Colombia, Costa Rica, and Puerto Rico.

His recordings of Joaquin Rodrigo's Concierto de Aranjuez with conductor and tenor Placido Domingo and the Philharmonia Orchestra was cited as the best recording of that piece in Classic CD Magazine, while Cuba! was called "an extraordinary musical achievement" by *The San Francisco Chronicle*. His release, Concierto Barroco, with the Orquesta Sinfonica de Galicia and conductor Victor Pablo Perez, received a Latin Grammy nomination for Best Classical Recording. In 2007, Manuel Barrueco received a Grammy nomination for the "Best Instrumental Soloist Performance" for his *Solo Piazzolla*, which was the first recording on the exclusive *Manuel Barrueco Collection* on Tonar Music. (Preceding information from www.barrueco.com).

Jessica Aguirre is a first generation Cuban-American born in Miami who is an Emmy award winning television journalist. Jessica began her broadcasting career while a student at the University of Miami. While living in Florida, Aguirre was hired as a general assignment reporter for Fox affiliate WSVN. She was promoted to co-anchor for the station's 10:00 pm newscast, which also featured a young Jillian Warry reporting the weather.

Aguirre moved to Los Angeles where she worked at ABC owned-and-operated station KABC-TV as a reporter and anchor. After her work in Los Angeles, in the mid-1990s, Aguirre came to the San Francisco Bay area where she was hired by KGO-TV Channel 7. After leaving her KGO position, she was hired as an anchor for NBC owned-and-operated station KNTV Channel 11. She currently anchors the station's 6:00 pm and 11:00 pm newscasts, as well as the host of the Emmy nominated *NBC Class Action*. Aguirre has won Emmy awards for her reporting on migrant workers, and on child molestation, while working in Los Angeles and Miami.

Silvio Canto Jr. was born in Cuba and arrived with his family at age 12 in 1964 via Mexico and Jamaica. Eventually the family relocated to Madison, Wisconsin, where the frigid weather was offset by the warm reception they received from the locals. Silvio attended high school there and went on to earn a B.A. in Political Science from Towson State University in Maryland.

Canto is the owner and General Manager of the Canto Group, a recruiting firm specializing in working with Dallas-Fort Worth companies looking for bilingual talent such as plant managers and controllers. He also has extensive banking experience in the United States and Mexico.

Today Silvio is a media celebrity as the host and director of Canto Talk, a blog radio program that is transmitted nightly at 8 PM CST from Dallas, Texas. His show focuses on current events; among his many distinguished guests are authors Carlos Eire and Humberto Fontova, Richard Baehr of American Thinker, Dr. Ileana Johnson, among others. Canto recently published a memoir, *Cubanos in*

*Wisconsin*, that depicts his family's history in Cuba and their journey to the United States. It is a fascinating and engaging tale of how an immigrant family surpassed all odds and achieved the American Dream.

Angela Anais Juana Antolina Rosa Edelmira Nin y Culmell (1903- 1977) better known as Anais Nin, was a celebrated writer and diarist with a penchant for erotica. She was born in France; her father was composer Joaquin Nin, who grew up in Spain but was born and returned to Cuba. Her mother, Rosa Culmell y Vigaraud, was of Cuban, French, and Danish ancestry. Anais moved to the United States in 1914 after her father deserted the family. In the U.S. she attended Catholic schools, dropped out of school, worked as a model and dancer, and returned to Europe in 1923. She also lived for some time in Spain and Cuba.

She studied psychoanalysis with Otto Rank and briefly practiced as a lay therapist in New York. She was also a patient of Carl Jung for a time as well. Finding it difficult to get her erotic stories published, Anais Nin helped found Siana Editions in France in 1935. By 1939 and the outbreak of World War II she returned to New York, where she became a figure in the Greenwich Village crowd.

An obscure literary figure for most of her life, when her journals-kept since 1931- began to be published in 1966, Anais entered the public eye. The ten volumes of *The Diary of Anais Nin* have remained popular. These are more than simple diaries; each volume has a theme, and were likely written with the intent that they later be published. Letters she exchanged with intimate friends, including Henry Miller, have also been published. The popularity of the diaries brought interest in her previously published novels. *The Delta of Venus* and *Little Birds*, originally written in the 1940s, were published after her death (1977, 1979).

Anais Nin is known, as well, for her lovers, who included Henry Miller, Edmund Wilson, Gore Vidal and Otto Rank. She was married to Hugh Guiler of New York who tolerated her affairs. She also entered into a second, bigamous marriage to Rupert Pole in California. She had the marriage annulled about the time she was achieving more widespread fame. She was living with Pole at the time of her death, and he saw to the publication of a new edition of her diaries, unexpurgated.

The ideas of Anais Nin about "masculine" and "feminine" natures have influenced that part of feminist movement known as "difference feminism". She disassociated herself late in her life from the more political forms of feminism, believing that self-knowledge through journaling was the source of personal liberation. (Preceding information from womenshistory.about.com).

I realize some folks may be wondering why I haven't graced these pages with Cuban hunk and heartthrob William Levy...well, wonder no more. The handsome actor and model was born in Cuba in 1980 (his maternal grandfather was Jewish) and arrived in our shores when he was 15. As a youngster he dreamed of playing professional baseball but changed his mind once he began to act and model. He studied acting in both Miami and Los Angeles, where he moved to begin his acting career.

From the age of 22, this "hot, hot, hot Cuban hunk", as he was called in the gossip news when he was on "Dancing With The Stars", began doing bit parts in Miami for

Univision. He also began his modeling career, which led him to be hired in 2002 for two of the reality shows produced by Telemundo: *Isla de la Tentacion* (Isle of Temptation) and *Protagonistas de Novela* (Soap Stars).

In 2003, while appearing in *Protagonistas*, Levy met Mexican-American actress Elizabeth Gutierrez, and began an 8-year relationship with her. The couple has two children but ended their relationship in May 2011. In 2005 he starred in a play performed in San Juan, Puerto Rico, called *La Nena Tiene Tumbao*. He then moved on to Spanish-language soaps on Univision: *Olvidarte Jamas* (Forget You Never), *Mi Vida Eres Tu* (You Are My Life) and *Acorralada* (Cornered).

Levy's breakthrough Mexican soap operas on Televisa were *Pasion* (2007) and *Cuidado con el Angel* (Watch Out for the Angel) (2008), which first broadcast in June 2008 in Mexico, and in the U.S. in September of that year. It is reported that this soap averaged 45.7 million viewers per evening.

From as early as 2006, People en Español had a special interest in Levy, whose name appeared on their list of "Los 20 solteros mas sexys" (The 20 sexiest bachelors). For two years, 2008 and 2009, he was named by this magazine as one of "Los 25 hombres más guapos" The 50 best looking). In 2009 and again in 2011, he was listed as one of 'Los 25 hombres mas guapos" (The 25 handsomest men). Levy's face appeared on their 15th Anniversary cover in 2011, where he's called "El hombre mas sexy" (The sexiest man). In December 2012 Levy was cast as Captain Damian Fabre for the remake of *La Tormenta*, titled *La Tempestad* which is currently in production and is set to air in 2013. (Preceding information from william-levy.net).

Maria Argelia Vizcaíno came to the United States in 1980 and resides in West Palm Beach, Florida. She is well-known in the South Florida Cuban community as a multi-talented writer, historian, journalist, television producer and screenwriter. She has authored two books about Cuban culture and history, "Guanabacoa la Bella"and "Son y Sazon". She also has a large fan base who read her weekly column "Faranduleando con Maria Argelia" that offers insights into the lives of celebrities and artists.

On the literary front, she won third place in 1999 in the international literary contest Sociedad Cultural Santa Cecilia held in Miami-Dade County. In 2009, she was awarded second place in the I Concurso de Textos Humoristicos with her monologue 'El secreto de Mariam". In 2010, she participated in the Miami Book Fair (the nation's largest), where she presented her latest book, "Son y Sazon", a book about Cuban cuisine.

She developed a following with her column Estampa de Cuba, which was published in numerous newspapers and magazines across the United States and abroad. Some of her writings were also translated to Italian and Portuguese. In addition, Maria Argelia has worked as a radio co-host; she was the first salsa dance instructor in Palm Beach County from 1992 to 2009. The trailblazer was also the first in that part of Florida to write, direct and choreograph a musical review with multicultural, local talent. She became the first Hispanic woman in Palm Beach to write a history book with the publication of "Guanabacoa la Bella" (2006). Vizcaino is very grateful to the United States for the opportunity she has been given to live in freedom and be able to express herself as she chooses; in

her web site mariaargeliavizcaino.com she includes a link
titled I Love USA.

# Sports Figures

In my previous book, *The Cubans Our Legacy in the United States*, I profiled the following notable baseball players: Martin Dihigo, Jose Canseco, Rafael Palmeiro, Minnie Miñoso, Luis Tiant, Bert Campaneris, Adolfo Luque, Esteban Bellan, Tony Oliva, Tony Perez, and Major League managers Preston Gomez and Mike Gonzalez. The statistics provided below are from *Baseball References.com* and *Baseball Almanac*.

Cuban born Miguel Angel Cuellar Santana (May 8, 1937- April 2, 2010) better known as Mike Cuellar, was an outstanding left-handed pitcher who played 15 years in the Major Leagues. He was feared for his deceptive screwball that baffled opposing hitters for years. His achievements on the mound were impressive: a pitching record of 185 wins, 130 losses, with an excellent 3.14 ERA. Cuellar was a 4 time All Star and was voted into the Baltimore Orioles' Hall of Fame. He also played for the Cincinnati Reds, St. Louis Cardinals, Houston Astros, and California Angels.

His greatest season was in 1969, when he became the first Baltimore hurler to win the Cy Young Award (honoring the league's best pitcher), sharing it with Denny

McLain of the Detroit Tigers. Cuellar became also the first Latin American pitcher to receive the "Cy Young Award." During that season his record was 23 wins, 11 losses with 5 shutouts. His pitching prowess helped the Orioles reach three straight World Series appearances from 1969-1971. In 1970 Cuellar won a career best 24 games while losing just 8 and hit a grand slam home run in Game 1 of the ALCS. He is the only pitcher to have accomplished that feat during the playoffs. He then proceeded to beat Cincinnati in Game 5 to capture the World Series title for the Orioles. Although he gave up three runs in the first inning of that game, he allowed just two hits the rest of the game to secure the victory.

Leo Cardenas, born Leonardo Lazaro Cardenas Alfonso, was known as "Mr. Automatic" and "Chico" during his 16 year career in the Major Leagues. He was considered one of the best fielding shortstops of his era for his wide range in reaching ground balls. He played 9 seasons with the Cincinnati Reds and also with the Minnesota Twins, California Angels, and Texas Rangers. Cardenas was a 5 time All Star and a Gold Glove winner in 1965. During his career he accumulated a .257 BA, with 118 HRs and 689 RBIs. He won the starting shortstop position in 1962 and hit for a .294 average, 10 home runs and 60 RBIs.

He remained the Reds' starting shortstop for 7 seasons, was selected to the All Star game in 1964, 1965, and 1968, and picked to start in 1966. He had 8 RBIs and hit 4 home runs in a double header against the Chicago Cubs on June 5, 1966 on his way to setting a club record for round trippers by a shortstop with 20 (later broken by Hall of Famer Barry Larkin). In 1969 he was traded to Minnesota and batted .280 with 10 homers and 70 RBIs while hitting at the bottom of the batting order. He also tied an AL record for assists by a shortstop with 570. Cardenas was batting .285 with 11 home runs and 46 RBIs at the 1971 All Star break to be named to his only AL All Star team.

He finished that year with 18 home runs, 75 RBIs and a stellar .985 fielding percentage to receive the Calvin R. Griffith Award given each season to the team's Most Valuable Player. As of this writing Cardenas resides with his family in Cincinnati, Ohio and participates in numerous Reds' community activities.

Camilo Pascual was another formidable pitcher who began his major league career with the Washington Senators in 1954 at the age of 20. The Havana right-hander played 18 years with the Senators, Minnesota Twins, Cincinnati Reds, Los Angeles Dodgers, and Cleveland Indians. He compiled a record of 174 wins, 170 losses and a fine 3.63 ERA. Those who follow baseball marvel how many of those losses he would have won if his team had scored more runs when he was pitching. He played in an era when starting pitchers where expected to finish a game; in all he pitched 132 completed games and twice led the league in complete games, 18 (1962, 1963).

Pascual's best seasons where in 1962 when he recorded 20 wins, 11 losses, 3.32 ERA with 18 complete games and 5 shutouts; and in 1963 he went 21-9 with a sparkling 2.46 ERA, again with 18 complete games and 3 shutouts. Ironically, in 1961 he threw 8 shutouts with a 3.46 ERA but his record was only 15-16. He was a 5 time All Star selection, and in the 1961 All Star Game he hurled 3 hitless innings and struck out 4 batters. Pascual led the American League in strikeouts in 1961 (221), 1962 (206), and 1963 (202). In the 1959 season (before the designated hitter rule) he batted a remarkable .302 in 86 at bats. He was also a fine defensive player, finishing his career with a fielding percentage of 97.3%.

From 1978-1980 Pascual was the Minnesota Twins pitching coach. Since 1989, he has worked as international scout for the Oakland Athletics, New York Mets, and the Los Angeles Dodgers. In 1983 he was elected to the Cuban Baseball Hall of Fame (author's note: since 1960 Cuba does not induct players based in the U.S., the Cuban Baseball Hall of Fame mentioned here is in the U.S.): then in 1996 he was inducted into the Caribbean Baseball Hall of Fame as part of its first class. On May 10, 2010 he was elected in the inaugural class of the Latino Baseball Hall of Fame in the Dominican Republic. Finally, on July 15, 2012 he was inducted into the Twins Hall of Fame.

Sandy Amorós (January 30, 1930-June 27, 1992) was an outfielder for the Brooklyn and Los Angeles Dodgers and Detroit Tigers from 1952 until 1960. His career statistics were modest: a .255 batting average, with 43 home runs and 180 runs batted in. But he is remembered (undoubtedly by New York Yankees fans) by a memorable catch he made in Yankee Stadium in the sixth inning of the decisive Game 7 of the 1955 World Series. The defensive gem is arguably the second best in post season baseball after Willie Mays' "The Catch" during the 1954 World Series between the New York Giants and the Cleveland Indians.

This was the scenario: The Dodgers were winning 2-0 and Amoros was brought in as a defensive replacement in left field. The first two batters in the inning reached base and the dangerous Yogi Berra, known for hitting balls out of the strike zone, connected on a shot toward the left field corner that looked like a sure double, as most of the outfield had shifted right against the left-hitting Yankees catcher. Film replays show Amoros seemingly coming out of nowhere, extending his gloved right hand to catch the ball and immediately skidded to a stop to avoid crashing into the fence near Yankee Stadium's 301 feet distance marker in the left field corner. He then threw to the relay man, shortstop Pee Wee Reese, who in turn threw to first baseman Gil Hodges, doubling Gil McDougald off first; Hank Bauer grounded out to end the inning and the Dodgers won the Series.

After the 1960 season Amoros returned to Cuba and immediately ran afoul with the Castro regime. He refused to take the manager's job at the despot's request for the Cuban National Team. As reported in *SI Vault*, Castro, not used to be spurned, stripped Amoros of the $30,000 ranch that he owned in Cuba, car, all his assets, and cash. He was detained in Cuba and not permitted to report for the 1962 Mexican League season. The article quotes that Amoros told the *The Sporting News*, "I don't like the guy. I thought he was loco. When I refused to manage, that's when the trouble started". Compared to the thousands who have been executed for not agreeing with the dictator, Sandy got off rather easy. Eventually, five years later in 1967, he was permitted to leave the country for the United States.

His life in the United States was not easy, his wife divorced him and he was left poor and alone. He eventually moved in with his best friend, Victor Germain from Puerto Rico who lived in Central Florida. He lost his buddy in 1986, then lost part of his left leg in 1987 to circulatory problems and gangrene. During this difficult period old teammates and the Baseball Assistance Program helped him out. Five years later, at age 62, Sandy Amoros died from pneumonia in Miami, Florida. Sadly, he had been scheduled to travel to Brooklyn for a day in his honor and an appearance with Yogi Berra at a baseball-card show.

Rey Ordoñez became in 1993 the second Cuban baseball player in history to defect to the United States. On July 10, 1991, pitcher Rene Arocha was the first to defect from the Cuban national team. Ordoñez, a shortstop, played nine seasons for the New York Mets, Tampa Bay Rays, and Chicago Cubs.

Although his career batting average was mediocre at best (.246), he was defined as an exceptional defensive player. Ordoñez went on to win three consecutive Gold Glove Awards with the Mets (1997, 1998, and 1999). During the 1999 and 2000 seasons, he set a Major League record for shortstops by playing 101 consecutive games without committing a fielding error. Additionally, in 1999, Ordoñez made only 4 errors while posting a .994 fielding percentage, a performance that one could argue may be the best defensive season ever by a Major League shortstop. From 1996 to 2000, Rey Ordoñez was considered the best defensive shortstop in the Major Leagues.

Osvaldo Alonso is a midfielder with the Seattle Sounders FC in Major League soccer. He began his career in Pinar del Rio in Cuba after which he defected to the United States in June, 2007. Initially Alonso trained with Chivas USA and was offered a $12,900 developmental contract with the team. Eventually he opted to sign with

Charleston Battery on the assumption he would get more playing time on a USL First Division team.

He impressed early after a strong outing in the preseason Carolina Challenge Cup 2008, and ultimately enjoyed an impressive rookie season in which he started 31 games for the Battery and scored 7 goals. He was named 2008 team MVP and Newcomer of the Year on fan votes, the team's Player's Player of the Year by a team vote, and the USL-1 Rookie of the Year by league coach and GM vote.

Alonso was signed by the Seattle Sounders where he quickly became a regular starter at defensive midfield, being voted team MVP in 2010 and 2011. On June 19, 2012, he became a citizen of the United States and he stated he would like to play for the United States national team despite playing for Cuba in the past.

So how did Alonso defect? He was in Houston, Texas with the Cuban national team waiting to play the Honduran selection. On an outing to Wal-Mart, while his countrymen were busy browsing through merchandise, he quietly slipped away and walked several blocks from the store until he found someone who spoke Spanish. He then borrowed a cell phone and called a friend in Miami. Aside from saving money and living better, at Wal-Mart one can also find freedom.

Zoilo Versalles (December 18, 1939- June 9, 1995) was a Major League shortstop who played for the Washington Senators, Minnesota Twins, Los Angeles Dodgers, Cleveland Indians, Atlanta Braves and Hiroshima Toyo Carp in Japan. His career statistics were average at best: .242 batting average, 95 home runs, and 471 runs batted in. His professional accomplishments include being selected to the All-Star Game in 1963 and 1965 and winning twice the Gold Glove for his position (1963, 1965).

Versalles is probably the most obscure recipient of the American League Most Valuable Player award, achieved in 1965. During that season he batted .273, with 126 runs scored, 45 doubles, 12 triples, and 122 strikeouts, all league-leading statistics. He was also picked as an All-Star and won a Gold Glove. The runner-up for the MVP award was a team mate and fellow Cuban, Tony Oliva.

Unfortunately for Versalles in subsequent years his weak hitting was compounded with poor fielding; he lead the American League in errors during 1965-1967. During his most productive seasons (1961-1965) he lead all AL shortstops with 76 home runs. Versalles went down in history as the first Latin American player to be named Most Valuable Player in the American League. This writer saw Zolio Versalles play against the New York Yankees in the Bronx a few times. As a die hard Yankees and Mickey Mantle fan, I would suffer as the Twins would batter my beloved Bronx Bombers on their way to the World Series.

Luis Sarria (1911- 1991) is best known in boxing as Muhammad Ali's personal physical conditioner, masseur and corner man for all of Ali's pro career bouts. Sarria had been a fighter and trainer in his native Cuba until the communist government outlawed professional boxing. He then sought asylum and moved to Miami where he soon found work.

In Miami, Sarria started life anew. He was flat broke, an exile in a strange land but he had a good reputation as an honest trainer and he had a friend in Angelo Dundee.

The Dundee brothers had spent over a decade importing and exporting Cuban fighters for their Miami Beach cards. Angelo spoke broken Spanish and his gym was full of new exile boxers: Luis Rodriguez, Florentino Fernandez, Jose Napoles, Angel Robinson Garcia, to name a few.

Sarria and Ali developed a rather interesting relationship. Sarria only learned a few phrases of English and Ali could muster a few words in Spanish, but their language differences did not prevent both men from becoming friends, using their own sign language to communicate. Sarria became Ali's conditioner, training the Great One, running him through endless hours of sit ups and knee bends, tuning his body while Dundee prepared the strategy for the upcoming bouts. Ferdie Pacheco, the famed Fight Doctor, said this of Sarria: "His conditioning allowed for no mistakes, not even Ali could con him (Sarria) out of exercises".

Dundee added: "Ali couldn't pull anything on Sarria, because Sarria wouldn't stand for it. In Muhammad's later years, Sarria was the one that kept fat off his body."(Preceding information taken from boxrec.com, cyberboxingzone.com).

Ralph Ortega was born in Cuba and arrived in Miami with his family as young boy. He was a star linebacker at Coral Gables High School in Coral Gables, Florida and attended the University of Florida on a football scholarship where he played from 1971 to 1974. He became a hero when in 1973 he helped the Florida Gators beat the Auburn Tigers for the first time at Jordan-Hare Stadium in fourteen visits. Ortega's big play was a crushing tackle that caused a fumble by Auburn's tailback inside the Gator's five yard line before halftime. The Gators won 12-8, with Auburn's only points near the end of the game.

Ortega finished his college career with 357 tackles, twelve forced fumbles (eight recovered), and five interceptions. He was a first-team All-Southeastern Conference (SEC) selection in 1973 and 1974, a first-team All-American in 1974, an Academic All-American, and the team captain during his senior year. He graduated from Florida with a B.A. in Management and was inducted into the University of Florida Athletic Hall of Fame as a "Gator Great" in 1978.

Ralph played six years in the National Football League. He was chosen in the second round (twenty-ninth pick overall) of the 1975 draft by the Atlanta Falcons. He was a starting linebacker in 1977, and a key part of the renowned "Gritz Blitz" Falcons defense. He was traded to the Miami Dolphins for a future third-round draft pick in 1979. He then finished his career with the Dolphins in 1980. In 2007, thirty-six years after he graduated from high school, the Florida High School Athletic Association (FHSSA) recognized Ortega as one of the "100 Greatest Players of the First 100 Years" of Florida high school football.

Jim Larrañaga is the University of Miami's basketball coach who led the team to a surprising Sweet Sixteen berth during the 2013 NCAA basketball championship. Although the Hurricanes did not advance, under his leadership the team surpassed all expectations, having being ranked as high as second nationally. As noted in an article in *The Miami Herald* dated March 22, 2013, according to Larrañaga, his grandfather was born in Cuba and was part of the Por Larrañaga Cigar Company. Jim's father moved to New York and wanted his kids to Americanize, this meant not learning Spanish and pronouncing the last name with an extra-nasally American "a", thus eliminating the tilde pronunciation.

Larrañaga's success this past season was recognized and he was voted National Coach of the Year. He was also named Coach of the Year by his fellow coaches in the Atlantic Coast Conference. The coach was also an outstanding shooting guard/small forward at Providence College. He led the team in scoring his sophomore and junior seasons, at 19.4 and 16.3 points per game. Perhaps his most impressive accomplishment was when he scored 47 points against Julius Erving's team in the Port Chester, N.Y., tournament, a pro-am event played in a small Catholic high school gym. Erving had just turned pro, and Larrañaga had just graduated from Providence.

The Bronx native was drafted by the Detroit Pistons in the sixth round of the 1971 draft but wound playing in Belgium and then turned to coaching. His first head coaching opportunity was at American International College, a Division II program. From there he coached at Bowling Green for 11 years, leaving the school as the second-winningest head coach in school history. At George Mason Larrañaga achieved 271 wins, making him the Colonial Athletic Association's and the school's winningest coach. In 2006 he led George Mason University to the Final Four. Under him the 2013 Hurricanes won the ACC Championship, the first tournament title in the program's history, finishing the season with a record of 29 victories and only 7 defeats.

What's a Miami boy doing speed skating on ice? For Eddy Álvarez, this has been his passion since he laced up his skates at four years of age. At four he was already national champion in his category and had earned the nickname of Eddy the Jet for his blazing speed on the ice. An article in *el Nuevo Herald* chronicles the young athlete's exploits. As of this writing (February 2013), he is in full training for the upcoming world championships in Budapest, Hungary. The twenty-three year old aspires to medal in the 500 and 1500 meters in Short Track competition. His ultimate goal is to participate in the Winter Olympic Games in 2014 to be held in Sochi, Russia. He would be the second Cuban-American from Miami to participate, following trailblazer Jennifer Rodriguez. In 2009 as a member of the Junior World Team he won a Gold medal in the 3K relay, in 2013 he achieved 4th place in the U.S. Championships.

Eddy's father recalled that Eddy would train once a week and win every meet against skaters from colder climates who practiced daily. He won four national titles in different age categories but he was torn between his passion for the ice and his other love, baseball. He attended baseball powerhouse Columbus High School and was an outstanding shortstop whom some scouts considered a major league prospect. During his four years there he hardly put on his skates. His older brother Nick was one of the best prospects with the Los Angeles Dodgers and his father, like a good Cuban *papi*, dreamed of having two sons play in the Majors. But for now Eddy is concentrating on his immediate desire to be part of the U.S. Winter Olympic team and ultimately, an Olympic champion.

After graduating from secondary school he packed his bags, bid farewell to sunny South Florida and moved to

Salt Lake City to prepare for the event in Hungary. After a few months he suffered injuries in both knees that required surgery in March of 2012. His physicians advised him not to skate for some time to allow his knees to heal so Eddy enrolled in a junior college in Utah and began playing baseball. In a short period he became one of the best collegiate shortstops and scouts wanted to sign him to a Major League contract. But he kept putting them off because he wanted to return to the ice. His recovery lasted shorter than expected and Eddy is back on the national team waiting to showcase his speed to the world.

Amy Joy Rodríguez, whose paternal grandparents were from Cuba and immigrated to the United States in the 1950s, is a soccer player who plays for Seattle Reign FC in the National Women's Soccer League and is also a member of the United States women's national soccer team. She previously played professionally for the Boston Breakers and the Philadelphia Independence of the WPS.

Ms. Rodriguez attended high school in Rancho Santa Margarita, California where she was a Parade All-American in 2003 and 2004 and the Gatorade Player of the Year in 2005. In that same year Amy was considered the nation's top recruit and was named National Player of the Year by Parade Magazine, EA Sports and NSCAA after scoring 17 goals in 15 games for Santa Margarita High during her senior year. She earned local honors as the Orange County Register Player of the Year and Girls Soccer Player of the Year, as well as the *Los Angeles Times'* Girls' Soccer Player of the Year.

She played as a forward during the 2008 Beijing Olympics and started four of five games, where she scored against New Zealand. Amy had appeared in 18 senior team matches going into the Olympics. She provided the assist on Carli Lloyd's game-winning goal in the first period of extra time in the Gold medal match to clinch the title. Rodriguez scored five goals in a 2012 CONCACAF Olympic qualifying game between the United States and the Dominican Republic, the final score was 14-0. Her performance set a record for goals scored in a single match by one player in CONCACAF Olympic qualifying and tied the single-game record for the U.S. national team. She was a member of the team that competed in the 2012 London Olympics. She played four matches as a substitute and received her second Olympic Gold medal, after the team won Gold at the 2008 Beijing Games.

Gilbert Arenas is a professional basketball player whose grandfather was born in Cuba. One of Gilbert's cousins is Javier Arenas, a professional football player who plays cornerback with the Kansas City Chiefs. Gilbert attended high school in California and accepted a scholarship offer to the University of Arizona. He entered the 2001 National Basketball Association draft and was selected in the second round (30th pick) by the Golden State Warriors. He has also suited up for the Washington Wizards, Orlando Magic, and Memphis Grizzlies. Since 2012 he has played with the Shanghai Sharks of the Chinese Basketball Association.

Arenas is a three time NBA All-Star selection and was honored as the NBA's Most Improved Player in 2003. He was also the NBA's Rookie Challenge MVP (2003), All-NBA Second Team (2007) and twice All-NBA Third Team (2005-2006).

Dara Torres, the daughter of Edward Torres, a Cuban-born casino owner, and former model Marylin Kauler, is an American international swimmer and a 12-time Olympic medalist. She is the first U.S. swimmer to compete in five Olympic Games- 1984, 1988, 1992, 2000 and 2008.

At age 41, she became the oldest swimmer ever to earn a place on the U.S. Olympic team at the 2008 Summer Olympics where she competed in the 50-meter freestyle, the 4x100-meter medley relay and the 4x100-meter freestyle relay, and won Silver medals in all three events.

Torres' 12 Olympic medals include four Gold, four Silver, and four Bronze. She won five of the medals in the 2000 Summer Olympics. She is tied with Jenny Thompson for the most medals won by a U.S. female swimmer, according to the *Los Angeles Times*. During a competition in the summer of 2012 in Omaha, Torres finished fourth in the 50-meter freestyle with a time of 24.82. Soon after, she announced her retirement from competitive swimming. (Preceding information from www.hispanicbusiness. com).

Aric Almirola was born in Tampa, Florida in 1984 and is a NASCAR Sprint Cup Series racecar driver, currently driving the no. 43 Smithfield Foods/United States Air Force/STP Ford for Richard Petty Motorsports. Almirola began racing when he was eight years old, racing Go-Karts. At 14, he began racing nationally. He won the pole position in his debut in the World Karting Association race and finished fourth in the standings that year. Two years later he moved up into modifieds and won several Rookie of the Year awards.

In 2003, Aric moved to the NASCAR Sun Belt Weekly Racing Division and finished second in the Rookie of the Year standings. He followed that up with five pole positions in 2003. In 2004, he became one of the first drivers to participate in NASCAR's Drive for Diversity program. He also signed with Joe Gibbs Racing as a development driver under a partnership with former NFL player Reggie White. Almirola ran the season at Ace Speedway, and won two races before finishing 11$^{th}$ in the point standings. He won five more races at the track in 2005, and made his Truck Series debut with Morgan-Dollar Motorsports and had two top ten in four races.

After leaving Joe Gibbs Racing, Almirola joined Dale Earnhardt, Inc. In 2010, he was to drive full time for Phoenix Racing no. 09 Cup series Chevrolet Impala. After departing Phoenix Racing he began to focus on his Truck Series ride. Almirola won his first race in the Camping World Truck Series at Dover International Speedway and won again at Michigan International Speedway.

Albertin Aroldis Chapman de la Cruz, better known as Aroldis Chapman, is a pitcher for the Cincinnati Reds. He pitched for Holguin in the "Cuban National Series" and internationally for the Cuban national baseball team before he defected from his birth land in 2009. He signed a contract with the Reds in 2010 and made his Major League debut that season.

As a relief pitcher, the left-hander won the MLB Delivery Man of the Month Award as the best relief pitcher for July 2012. As of August 2012, he holds the record for the fastest pitch speed in MLB history, after throwing a 105.1 mph fastball in 2010. He was also clocked by one radar gun at 106 mph in a later game, although this speed is disputed.

Chapman successfully defected while in Rotterman, Netherlands where the Cuban national team was participating in the World Port Tournament on July 1, 2009. He walked out of the front door of the team hotel and entered into an automobile driven by a friend. Chapman eventually established residency in Andorra and petitioned MLB to be granted free agent status. The Reds announced that they had signed Chapman to a six- year contract, worth $30.25 million according to MLB sources. The Associated Press reported that the bonus totals $16.25 million, paid annually over 11 years with an additional bonus if he became eligible for salary arbitration in 2012 or 2013.

He made his Major League debut on August 31, 2010, in the eighth inning against the Milwaukee Brewers; his first pitch (a strike) was clocked at 98 miles per hour, the catcher immediately tossed the ball into the dugout as a memento. On July 1, 2012 Chapman was named to his first All-Star Game. He won the MLB Delivery Man of the Month Award for July, 2012, in which he recorded 13 saves while not allowing a run in fourteen and a third innings while striking out 31 batters-more than 60% of the hitters he faced. It was the third month of the season in which he did not allow a single run. He was named the August Delivery Man of the Month as well.

Chapman completed the 2012 season with a record of 5 wins, 5 loses, with a 1.51 ERA and 38 saves, recording 122 strikeouts and 22 walks in 71.2 innings pitched. He had an amazing ratio of 15.3 strikeouts per 9 innings. Not only does he pitch fast, but he does the same when driving.

Chapman has received 6 speeding tickets in the U.S. and his driver's license was suspended after his last infraction.

Ryan Lochte is a multi-Gold medal winner in men's swimming for the United States Olympic team. He was born to a Cuban mother, Ileana, a native of Havana and a father of German and English descent. His family lived in Canandaigua, New York, but moved to Florida so his father could coach swimming. Ryan was taught to swim at the age of five by both of his parents.

He attended the University of Florida where he was the NCAA Swimmer of the Year twice, a seven-time NCAA Champion, a seven-time SEC Champion, and a twenty-four time All-American. At the 2006 NCAA Men's Swimming and Diving Championships, Lochte won individual titles in all three of his individual events, setting U.S. Open and American records in the 200-yard individual medley and the 200-yard backstroke. He also broke Tom Dolan's nearly decade-old NCAA record in the 400-yard individual medley.

During the 2004 Athens Games he won Gold in the 4x200 m freestyle relay and Silver in the 200 m individual medley. Four years later during the Beijing Olympics he achieved Gold in the 200 m backstroke with a world record time of 1:53.94; he also won Gold in the 4x200 m freestyle relay establishing a new record of 6:58.56. He closed the Games in China by winning Bronze in both the 200 m and 400 m individual medleys.

The 2012 London Olympics was another milestone for Lochte. He was awarded Gold medals in the 400 m individual medley and the 4x200 m freestyle relay. He also took Silver in both the 200 m individual medley and the

4x100 m freestyle relay. His last medal was Bronze in the 200 m backstroke. His five medals brought his total to 11 Olympic medals, tied for second among male swimmers with fellow Americans Mark Spitz and Matt Biondi, behind only Michael Phelps. His seven individual Olympic medals are the second most in men's Olympic swimming. Lochte has announced he plans to continue swimming through the 2016 Olympics in Rio de Janeiro.

Frank Mir, born in Las Vegas, is a mixed martial artist. He is a two time UFC Heavyweight Champion. He currently holds the record for most victories and submissions in the history of the UFC heavyweight division. Mir is also the only man in UFC history to win a bout by toe hold. Additionally, he holds the distinction of being the first and only man to both knock out and submit MMA legend Antonio Rodrigo Nogueira. Mir is the only fighter to submit former UFC Heavyweight Champion and WWE superstar Brock Lesnar and highly regarded Muay Thai striker Cheick Kongo. As of February 2013, Mir is ranked the #7 heavyweight in the world by Sherdog.

Mir's father is Cuban, born of Moroccan immigrants of Russian descent. It was his father who encouraged him to begin wrestling, on the basis that it could help him avoid submissions. He lost his first nine matches in his junior year in high school; as a senior he went 44-1 and won the state championship. And as they say, the rest is history.

One of the few Cuban-American professional tennis players is Christina McHale. She was born in 1992 in Teaneck, New Jersey to an Irish-American father and a Cuban mother. Her family lived in Hong Kong from the time she was three until she was eight, and she speaks

Mandarin Chinese with some fluency. In 2000, the family relocated to the United States and moved once again to New Jersey.

Christina currently trains at the USTA Training Center in Carson, California. At the age of 15, she left home to train at the USTA Training Center headquarters in Boca Raton, Florida. Her sister Lauren is a junior at UNC- Chapel Hill, where she plays tennis for the Tar Heels. Christina's highest ranking in singles play was #24 (August 20, 2012) and as of February 2013 she is ranked #49.

Frank Martin, born in Miami, is the current men's basketball coach for the University of South Carolina. Previously he was the head coach at Kansas State University, prior to that he was an assistant coach at the collegiate level and a head coach at Miami-area high schools. Martin graduated with a B.A. in Physical Education from Florida International University in 1993. He became well-known when he led Miami Senior High School to three consecutive state championships from 19996 to 1998. The last of those titles was later vacated due to recruiting violations involving school employees and boosters who gave housing assistance to some players. Although Martin was never personally accused of any wrongdoing, he was dismissed in 1999.

He joined the college ranks as an assistant coach/recruiting coordinator at Northeastern University from 2000 to 2004. He moved to the University of Cincinnati, serving one season each under Bob Huggins and Andy Kennedy. He then followed Huggins to Kansas State; on April 6, 2007, Martin was named head coach of the Wildcats in the wake of Huggins' resignation.

Martin's first season was marked by a number of firsts. The Wildcats were in the preseason Top 25 for the first time since 1972. The team then defeated the #10 Texas A&M on January 19, 2008, making the first win over a ranked team in nearly a year, as well as K-States' first victory over a Top 10 opponent since beating Texas in 2004. On January 30, 2008, Martin led Kansas State to victory over-then #2 Kansas, marking the Wildcats' first home win over their in-state rival since 1983. He led the 2007-2008 team to their first berth in the NCAA Tournament since 1996.

On March 2010, Martin led the Wildcats to the Elite Eight, their deepest run in the tournament since 1988. He was named the Big 12 Conference Men's Basketball Coach of the Year in 2010. On March 26, 2012, he sent a text message to ESPN confirming he had accepted the head coaching position at South Carolina. He compiled a record of 117 wins and 54 defeats at Kansas State. His first year at South Carolina was clearly a rebuilding phase, his team finished with 14 wins and 18 defeats.

Alberto Riveron, the National Football League's first Hispanic referee, was promoted in early 2013 to senior director of officiating. Riveron was born in Cuba and moved to Miami with his family at age 5. He became a referee in 2008 after serving as a side judge. He takes the newly created position as second in command of the department under new vice president of officiating Dean Blandino.

In his new job, Riveron will oversee the NFL's instant replay program and assist Blandino in assignment and evaluation of officials, and developing and distributing weekly training videos and other materials to improve accuracy and consistency. Riveron joins NFL Network vice president of human resources Andres Astralaga and Carolina Panthers coach Ron Rivera among Hispanics in high-ranking NFL positions. Riveron began officiating in Miami youth leagues in 1977. He made his college officiating debut in 1990, working primarily in the Big East and Conference USA. (Preceding information taken from espn.go.com).

I would be remiss if I did not include the seven Cuban women who played in a women's professional baseball league in the United States. The official name was All American Girls Professional Baseball League, but it was official for only two seasons. The original name was the All American Girls Softball League; this lasted until 1943, when the name was changed to the All American Girls Baseball League. In 1949 and 1950 the league was called the All American Girls Professional Baseball League and from 1951 to 1954 the league adopted American Girls Baseball League. Is everyone thoroughly confused now?

The League was owned by chewing gum mogul Philip K. Wrigley from 1943 to 1945, Arthur Meyerhoff from 1945 to 1951, and the teams were individually owned from 1951 to 1954. In 1947 and 1948, spring training exhibition games were held at the Gran Stadium in Havana, Cuba.

The seven *cubanitas* who played were Migdalia "Mickey" Pérez (1948-1954), Isabel Álvarez (1949-1964), Isora del Castillo (1949- 1951), Luisa Gallegos (1948- 1949), Mirtha Marrero (1948- 1953), Gloria Ruiz (1948-1949), and Zonia Vialat (1948). The most successful was Mickey Perez; she pitched a no-hitter (1953) and was single-season leader in complete games (1951), innings pitched (1951) and games pitched (1952). The ladies played for teams with delightful and distinctive feminine names such as, the Battle Creek Belles, Rockford Peaches, Kalamazoo Lassies, and Fort Wayne Daisies, among others.

In 1988, Mickey Perez became part of *Women in Baseball*, a permanent display based at the Baseball Hall of Fame and Museum in Cooperstown, New York, which was unveiled to honor the entire All American Girls Professional Baseball League. In 2011, Perez and her AAGP-BL teammates from Cuba were honored by having their names and photos presented at a ceremony in New York City. The event was organized by Leslie Heaphy, history professor at Kent State University of Ohio, during the Cuban Baseball Congress held at Fordham University.

# Entrepreneurs

An obituary column from December 2010 in *The Miami Herald* chronicles the life of entrepreneur Solomon Garazi. He was born June 3rd 1925 to Turkish and Syrian Jewish parents in Havana. He earned an Accounting degree from the University of Havana and married Esther Egozi in 1951. In 1960 he was forced to relinquish his business to the communist government, causing him to flee to Miami.

After 10 years of work in Miami, Solomon's family business, Suave Shoe Corp., became the first company owned by Cuban immigrants to be listed on the New York Stock Exchange. Deeply passionate for Israel and Latin American Jewry, his involvement with countless charitable organizations earned Solomon recognition as one of South Florida's most philanthropic Sephardic Jews. He was a principal founder of Temple Moses, his synagogue, the Miami Jewish Home and Hospital for the Aged, and South Florida branch of the Latin American Sephardic Federation.

Garazi was honored by many distinguished institutions, including the Jewish National Fund, the State of Israel Bonds Organization, the City of Miami Beach, the Mayor of Miami and the State of Florida. He was the first

"Jewban" to be named to the board of directors of the Greater Miami Jewish Federation.

In 1971 Gilbert de Cárdenas and his wife Jennie were able to obtain U.S. visas and left Cuba to start a new life in Los Angeles. The going was difficult at first, they arrived with three small children and expecting a fourth. A story in *Examiner.com* relates that Gilbert tasted the cheese sold in small Los Angeles markets and knew he could do better. The reason was because Gilbert had learned to make cheese from his father in Cuba. The enterprising immigrants scraped together their hard-earned savings of $1,500 and in 1973 founded Cacique Inc., a Spanish name signifying the chief of a tribe. During the early years Gilbert taught his wife how to make high quality fresh cheese, also known as queso fresco. He then sold and delivered the product with the help of the children after school and during summer vacation. After the first year they were able to hire their first employee.

Today their children run the company which is the largest fresh cheese maker in the United States that also sells the most chorizos in the marketplace. The family merged science and chemistry along with the state-of-the-art facilities that use the latest global cheese making and meat processing technology to create authentic old-world products. Cacique's products include high quality cheese, cream, chorizo, and yogurt. What started with the founders making 100 pounds of cheese a day in a tiny one-room facility has grown to become a top national brand with a modern 200,000 square-foot facility outside of Los Angeles. Estimated annual sales exceed $100 million dollars.

According to *Cheese Market News*, the company has taken a two-prong approach: expand knowledge of traditional Hispanic cheeses among the non-Hispanic consumer population while at the same time generate more excitement for its broadest base of customers, first-and-second generation Hispanic consumers in the United States. A key component, as described in the newspaper, is the company's new partnership with Food Network Celebrity Chef Aaron Sanchez to promote Cacique's product line.

Another way the company is seeking to reach its Hispanic consumers, as noted in the industry newspaper, is through its sponsorship of the Mexican National Soccer Team. The initiative, aimed at reaching the company's core Hispanic consumer audience, is utilizing radio, billboards and on-pack logos noting the sponsorship. The agreement with the team makes Cacique the presenting sponsor of all Mexican National Soccer Team games in the United States.

The company is also involved in the community it serves. Cacique employs hundreds of workers, most of Mexican origin. The Cacique Foundation is a family foundation that contributes to charities in the Los Angeles and Miami areas. Currently the foundation is working to improve community baseball fields. For every double play made by the Los Angeles Angels and the Los Angeles Dodgers, Cacique donates $100 to support baseball for disadvantaged youth.

An article dated April 19th, 2013, in *The Miami Herald* chronicles the life and death of Margarita Dosal, tobacco company president. She was known as the flamboyantly fancy, gleefully generous matriarch of a family that reestablished its Cuban tobacco company in Opa-Locka, Florida after fleeing the Castro regime. The note mentions that Dosal was a Cuban "steel magnolia" who rolled up her sleeves and went to work on the factory floor as her husband, his brother and father rebuilt Dosal Tobacco Corporation in 1962, she "won back our dignity and secured the future for her children and grandchildren," said daughter Beatriz Margarita Bolton of Great Britain.

Draped in diamonds and furs, every shimmering, coppery hair in place, Dosal took equal delight in piloting her Rolls Royce Phantom to a charity gala and to Disney World- with head-turning stops at Cracker Barrel and Dunkin' Donuts along the way. She treated her employees like family, covering 100 percent of their health-insurance costs, and treated her family like royalty, hosting lavish quinces and weddings for children and grandchildren.

Dosal and her late husband, Martin Roberto Dosal, married in 1951, "were Lucy and Ricky Ricardo," daughter Miriam Dosal Stone said. She adored children, and donated to Miami Children's Hospital, which last year named an oncology wing activities room in her honor. A maternity waiting room at Baptist Hospital also bears her name, and her family's foundation supports a school for AIDS orphans in Kenya. "She was beautiful, kind-hearted, very giving and a passionate children's advocate," said Lucy Morillo-Agnetti, President/CEO of Miami Children's Hospital Foundation. "Her legacy will forever be remembered through the Margarita C. Dosal Playroom".

Interestingly, Dosal was born in the U.S. to a Cuban military officer and his wife during a training stint at Fort Riley, Kansas, on March 6, 1931. She grew up in Havana, earned a Bachelor's degree in Education from Smith College in Massachusetts, taught kindergarten, then fled Cuba with three small children in 1959. "We were in New York when Batista fell," Miriam Stone recalled. "We went back to Cuba and gathered up a few things because they were sure they'd be going back".

Like so many others, the Dosals never did. But they had money in a New York bank, and were able to start over. After Martin Roberto died in 1992, his widow became president, holding 100 percent of the voting stock. Dosal markets the cigarette brands 305, DTC and Competidora in Florida and Texas, mainly at drug stores, mom-and-pop groceries and convenience stores. They generally sell for about $4 per pack, substantially less than premium brands, and aren't advertised beyond the point of sale. (Preceding information taken from www.miami-herald.com.)

Alexis Batista is a Miami-based architect and designer. Born in Banes, Cuba, he arrived at an early age to the United States with his parents. He is a graduate of the University of Miami with a Bachelors degree in Architecture and Fine Arts, with post-graduate studies in sculpture. He is a member of the American Institute of Architects (AIA) and the American Society of Interior Designers (ASID). His 20 years experience in architecture and interior design include the design and project management of large scale institutional and commercial projects, as well as high-end residential.

He founded Studio Alex Batista in 2004, with its main emphasis on interior architecture and design. Alexis has been the recipient of several design and art awards, most recently receiving the 2009 ASID Design Excellence Award for condominium/apartment design. His sculptural work and installations have been exhibited in private galleries and museums in South Florida. In addition, his work has appeared often in Miami Home & Décor as well as Luxe Magazine (Fall 2009).

The name Felipe Valls is synonymous with good eating in Miami. The highly successful entrepreneur celebrated in 2011 the 40th anniversary of the opening of Versailles Restaurant on Calle Ocho (S.W. 8th Street). His business was emblematic of the number of enterprises opened by Cuban Americans between 1972 and 1982-from 5,000 to 30,000. Valls had the vision of what this business could be; not only a restaurant chain to fulfill a basic need of Cuban Americans, but also a business that could grow, evolve and diversify.

Like most Cuban American business of the 1970s, Versailles Restaurant catered to a Cuban clientele. However, by the 1990s Versailles was attracting more diverse guests. The Cuban sandwich, the *cafecito* of Versailles and other delightful dishes became favorites of both Hispanics and non-Hispanics. Versailles became an obligatory destination for politicians, from candidates for local office to presidents of the United States. Just as important, the Valls family responded to market changes while retaining the pride and traditions of the Cuban American culture. This author can attest that on numerous occasions I have seen busloads of tourists march into the eatery to enjoy typical Cuban cuisine and then walk next door to Versailles Bakery to savor their home made *pastelitos* (pastries) and other calorie-filled sweets.

Today Felipe Valls must be proud of his legacy: 18 restaurants, including a location in Miami International Airport. For those who yearn to eat authentic Spanish food, then Casa Juancho is the place to eat in Little Havana, that fine establishment is also owned by Valls. Valls has taught his family well. His children and grandchildren have brought new ideas and opportunities to the business, and the patriarch has listened. The flourishing company employs 2,400 people from diverse origins. In my (and my wife's) humble opinion, the best *cortadito* in town is made at La Carreta (a chain owned by Valls) on Bird Road and 87th Avenue by Nilda... a charming Peruvian who works the cafeteria side of the restaurant. It is so good that we drive out of our way just to have our *cortadito* there. (Preceding information taken from republica.net).

Cuban-born Rosa Lowinger, Principal and Senior Conservator, is a Professional Associate of the American Institute for Conservation of Historic and Artistic Works since 1984. She holds a M.A. in Art History and Conservation from New York University's Institute of Fine Arts. With a focus in modern art and contemporary sculpture, architecture, and public art, Rosa has been in private practice in Los Angeles since 1988, serving such clients as the Broad Art Foundation, the Metropolitan Transit Authority Gold Line to Pasadena, the Hawaii State Foundation for Culture and the Arts, and the cities of Los Angeles, San Jose, Ventura, Santa Monica, Inglewood, Santa Fe Springs, and Honolulu.

Rosa lectures and publishes frequently on conservation topics related to modern and contemporary sculpture and architecture, and in 2009 was awarded the prestigious

Rome Prize in Conservation at the American Academy in Rome for research into the history of vandalism. She is the author of "Tropicana Nights: The Life and Times of the Legendary Cuban Nightclub" and a founding contributor to the award-winning art-and-culture blog c-monster.net. Rosa is particularly passionate about maintenance of the built heritage of Cuba, and actively seeks to promote international interest in its preservation.

Alex Meruelo was born in New York City and was raised in Los Angeles, California. He achieved a Bachelor of Science degree from California State University, Long Beach. He began his career in his father's tuxedo business and apparently business definitely "suits" him perfectly. Today Alex serves as the CEO and President of Meruelo Enterprises Inc., Cantamar Property Management Inc., and La Pizza Loca Inc. He has invested extensively in residential and commercial real estate throughout Southern California since 1987, primarily in Hispanic neighborhoods. Meruelo owns and manages over 1,000 residential units and over 20 retail units, and has overseen over 15 developments.

He established La Pizza Loca in 1986; today it has more than 50 locations in Southern California. Since 1999, he has focused his endeavors on the construction industry and, through Meruelo Enterprises, owns a number of established Southern California utility construction contractors including Herman Weissken Inc, Doty Bros .Equipment Co., and Tidwell Excavating. He serves as the Chairman of Herman Weissken, Inc. Mr. Meruelo serves as a Director of ExaDIGM, Inc., and Commercial Bank of California. He also owns Spanish-language television station KWHY-TV,

Grand Sierra Resort,, and other ventures. In 2011, Meruelo attempted to buy majority shares of the Atlanta Hawks professional basketball team but a deal could not be finalized. He would have been the first Latino owner of an NBA team.

Marcos A. Rodríguez is Founder and Managing Director of Palladium Equity Partners in New York City. He was six years old when his family fled communist Cuba; he is quoted as saying that his parents encouraged him to study because, "no one can take away your education". Marcos definitely followed his folks' advice: he holds an M.B.A. from The Wharton School of Business; a M.A. in International Studies from the Lauder Institute of the University of Pennsylvania, and a B.S. in Mechanical Engineering from Columbia University. He also graduated from GE's Manufacturing Management Program.

Before founding his firm Rodriguez was an investment banker who specialized in manufacturing. At Joseph Littlejohn & Levy-a private partnership that invests in corporate divestitures and in businesses that are consolidating-his deals included the creation of the world's dominant maker of car wheels, Hayes Wheels International Inc. In another deal, he assembled a new company using four parts plants purchased from General Motors Corporation.

The young entrepreneur is now on the lookout for other business opportunities. Marcos spearheaded some of Palladium's major investments, including Liberty Broadcasting and Fairfield Manufacturing. Palladium Equity Partners primarily invests in companies located in the United States Hispanic Market along with Mexico, Spain, and Brazil. It seeks to make equity investment between

$15 million and $75 million in companies generating revenue between $25 million and $500 million with EBITDA (earnings before interest taxes depreciation and amortization) between $5 million and $40 million. (Preceding information from mycrains.crainsnewyork.com).

Miguel "Mike" Fernandez, Chairman and CEO at Healthcare Acquisition Corp, also serves as the Chairman and CEO at CPHP Holdings Inc., and is the Chairman at MBF Healthcare Partners, L.P., is a Miami entrepreneur. He has the big office in a high rise, complete with plush furnishings, a big flat-screen TV, and photos of him with famous people. He has a helicopter, a corporate jet, and had a yacht, but he's having a new one built.

Fernandez has a portfolio of health care companies and a knack for coming out on top. What else can you say about a Cuban immigrant who came to the U.S. as a boy, became a paratrooper for three years; moved to Miami, lived in modest apartments, started out as a salesman, and, despite not having a college degree, found a way to become a multimillionaire? Somewhere along the line, he figured out the American Dream and he figured it out well.

One of his specialties is founding companies, shaping them up, and eventually selling them off for big money. His current roster of businesses includes a controlling interest in Navarro Discount Pharmacies, the largest retail pharmacy chain in the U.S. focused on the Hispanic market. Not that he's all about money. One of the things he likes about health care is the idea of helping people, including a unique insurance plan he and his partners started that exclusively serves HIV/AIDS patients. In the Mike Fernandez tradition, he is doing it big, getting NBA

Hall of Famer Ervin "Magic" Johnson, the world's most famous HIV-positive person, to buy into the venture and be a spokesperson for the company.

Fernandez has given away more money (he says $100 million over the last decade) than ordinary millionaires dream of making. For example, on September 2011, The Miguel B. Fernandez Family Foundation announced a donation of $5 million to Miami Children's Hospital Foundation for the creation of a revolutionary new trauma center as part of the new emergency department at Miami Children's Hospital. The trauma center expansion will allow the hospital to accommodate the growing number of patients from South Florida, Latin America and the Caribbean who rely on Miami Children's Hospital in their greatest time of need. (Preceding information from www.miamitodaynews.com).

Remedios Díaz- Oliver is the Miami-based President of All American Containers, Inc., a leading supplier in the United States of glass, plastic and metal containers and caps with operations in Miami, Tampa, Mexico, Puerto Rico, Atlanta and Dallas. Its marketing network spans to 50 countries in Central and South America, the Caribbean, Europe, Asia, Africa, Australia and New Zealand. The company was founded by Remedios Diaz-Oliver in 1991. As President and Chief Executive Officer, Mrs. Diaz-Oliver is entrusted with full administrative and financial responsibilities including financial statements.

Mrs. Diaz-Oliver is a former member of the Board of Directors of Avon Products, Inc., and Barnett Bank (Bank of America). She is a member of the Board of Directors of The Round Table, American Cancer Society, Cuban

Liberty Council, U.S. Cuba Democracy PAC, The Florida Council of 100 and Emeritus Director of U. S. West Inc. in Denver. She was also a member of the Board of Trustees of The Public Health Trust and Mercy Hospital.

She was selected as Outstanding Woman of the Year by the American Red Cross; Outstanding Woman of the Year by the Miami City Ballet; Business Woman of the Year by the Latin Chamber of Commerce; Entrepreneur of the Year by the Inter-American Businessmen's Association; Business Woman of the Year by the U.S. Hispanic Chamber of Commerce; Established Business-Owner of the Year by the National Association of Women Business Owners. Mrs. Diaz-Oliver was the first woman to receive the 'E" award (for excellence in exporting) from the President of the United States and the only Florida woman to be a member of the Board of Directors of three Fortune 500 companies, simultaneously. (Preceding information taken from business.fiu.edu).

*Automotive News* (March 5, 2012) profiles the life and accomplishments of entrepreneur Gus Machado. The publication relates that the last time Gus set foot in his native Cuba, in January 1960, he sold two used Chevrolets he had ferried across from Florida: a 1950 and a 1951. As he was standing in a Havana post office waiting to change into cash the money orders he had received for the cars, a rumor swept through the building that Fidel Castro was approaching the city and that he would change the country's currency. Machado got his money; then hurried for the ferry to Key West. He has not returned.

Machado, now a robust 78, still puts in 12 to 15 hour days every day at his two Miami-area Ford dealerships.

"Gus Machado is the North American success story", says Bill Wallace, owner of the Wallace Automotive Group in Stuart, Florida, which includes a Lincoln store. "I love what Gus represents and what he's done. Everybody who knows him reveres him. He is an entrepreneur's entrepreneur".

In 1949, Machado first moved to the United States to attend Edwards Military Institute in North Carolina and Greenville College in Greenville, Ill. He then lived in Joliet, Ill., and worked for Caterpillar Tractor Co. before moving to Miami in 1956. Starting with a gas station in 1956, Machado owned a series of used-car dealerships until he acquired his first franchise in 1982 with a store called Gus Machado Buick.

In 1984, he sold the Buick store and bought Johnson Ford in Hialeah. The dealership is Gus Machado Ford of Hialeah; he bought a second Ford store, now known as Gus Machado Ford of Kendall. During his peak years before the recession, Gus Machado Ford of Hialeah alone sold as many as 5,000 new and used vehicles per year. Since the downturn, he has struggled to get his numbers up again. In 2011, the two stores totaled 3,500 new and used cars.

Machado has become a major force in the world of South Florida philanthropy. His charitable activities take up a couple of single-spaced pages on the biographical sketch that appears on his dealership Web site, reflecting his having raised more than $2.5 million for local charities in the past 25 years. A lover of golf, Machado sponsors the annual Gus Machado Golf Classic, which benefits the American Cancer Society. He also organizes Calle Ocho, a Kiwanis event in Miami's Little Havana neighborhood that celebrates local culture.

During down times, Machado draws strength from a story that his grandfather, a farmer, told him long ago when Machado was a little boy on the family farm near Cienfuegos, Cuba. His grandfather told the young boy to look at the field and the trees around the field and to think about the cycle of life on the storm-based tossed island.

"He said that sometimes a hurricane comes around, and you go look at your field and you can only see one or two trees left standing. He told me: 'Do you know why they are still standing? It's because they had good roots'.

"If you got good roots, you have a good chance to make it".

Florida Crystals Corporation is a privately owned and diversified agriculture, consumer products, real estate, and energy enterprise. The company is a leading sugar producer and the United States' first fully integrated cane sugar company, harvesting its own sugar from the fields to consumers' homes. In Palm Beach County, Florida, the company owns 155,000 acres of land, two sugar mills, a sugar refinery, a rice mill, a packaging and distribution center, and a renewable energy facility.

The company is America's first and only domestic producer of certified organic sugar, grown and harvested in Florida. Florida Crystals also pioneered certified organic and natural rice production in the state. In addition, the company owns and operates the largest biomass power plant in North America, which produces eco-friendly energy that powers its operations and tens of thousands of homes.

The origins of Florida Crystals trace back five generations, when the Fanjul family began sugar farming and production in Cuba in the 1850s. After the communist takeover of Cuba, Alfonso Fanjul led the effort to reestablish the business in the rich and fertile soil of South Florida in 1960. Throughout the following decades, under the leadership of his sons Alfonso "Alfy" Fanjul and Jose "Pepe" Fanjul, the company has grown to be one of the largest, most innovative and successful agriculture companies in the world.

Today, along with its subsidiaries, as the world's largest sugar refiner, the company's production capacity exceeds 7 million tons of sugar per year with operations in Florida, California, Louisiana, New York, Maryland, Canada, Mexico, England and Portugal. Florida Crystals products are sold under the Domino, C&H, Florida Crystals, Redpath, Jack Frost, and Tate & Lyle brands. (Preceding information taken from floridacrystals.com).

As depicted in an article in *nytimes.com*, a Cuban refugee works hard and realizes the American Dream. Graciliano Rodríguez had been a wholesaler of potatoes and onions in Cuba until the Castro regime confiscated his business. Uncertain of the future, Rodriguez sent his children to the United States via Operation Pedro Pan. The family eventually reunited and started anew in Long Beach, California where Rodriguez went to work waiting tables and doing janitorial work on a second job.

Soon he found a way to work for himself in food distribution. In 1963 he opened a store in the Los Angeles produce market dealing in the kinds of beans, rice and peppers that people from Latin American favored. As of

2006, the 91 year old Rodriguez was still working daily at the warehouse complex in City of Industry, California that serves as headquarters for Mercado Latino Inc., a company run by his sons and daughter that has become one of the largest processors and distributors of Latin groceries and household goods to the nation's supermarket chains and Wal-Mart Stores.

Mercado Latino now has nine centers throughout the Western states for processing and distributing 3,500 products. It employs up to 400 full and part-time workers depending on seasonal needs and has more than $110 million in annual sales. In 1975 Rodriguez urged the children to buy one of the first I.B.M. System 32 minicomputers to upgrade Mercado Latino's accounting abilities. It was a huge risk because the computer cost more than the company was worth at that time, according to one of his sons. But using it allowed the family to take on more products and spread its operations from Texas to the Canadian border.

Author's note: In *The Cubans Our Legacy in the United States*, I profile other notable entrepreneurs and business leaders such as Roberto Goizueta (Coca Cola), Carlos Gutierrez (Kellogg Company), Jorge Perez (real estate magnate) and Gerry Grinberg (Movado) among others.

## The Pedro Pan Chapter

This section is about the young boys and girls who left Cuba under the auspices of Operation Pedro Pan. OPP was an organized effort by the Catholic Church that spirited about 14,048 children from the ages of 5 to 17 alone to the United States from 1960 until 1962. An eternal thanks to Monsignor Bryan O. Walsh, Ramon "Mongo" Grau Alsina and his sister Polita Grau ( they served respectively 20 and 14 years in Cuban jails for their participation in OPP), Jorge and Peggy Guarch and all others who coordinated our arrival to the United States. The Pedro Pan children were placed in foster homes, orphanages, Catholic institutions, or with close family members. Some waited less than a year, others 6 or more years before being reunited with their parents. In some cases the children lost their father or mother during the separation period. This author was 9 and his brother 11 when we arrived to this welcoming land on July 8, 1962. Our destiny was Florida City camp but we were fortunate that a cousin Ruby, and her husband, Luis Piriz, took us in. We lived with them the first nine months; then we moved to New York City with a maternal aunt and her wonderful husband who became our second parents. It was close to four years before we saw our parents again. The following profiles are a small sample of my fellow Pedro Pan brothers and sisters and their contributions to American society.

The founder and inspiration of Operation Pedro Pan Group was Elly Chovel, unfortunately she left us much too soon in 2007. She founded the organization to pay back the country that gave a home to her and more than 14,000 other unaccompanied children during Operation Pedro Pan between 1960 and 1962.

Elly was 16 and her sister 11 when they arrived in Miami, they were sent to Florida City Camp and soon were relocated with a family in Buffalo, New York. It took six years for the sisters to be reunited with their parents. Chovel wed Thomas F. Flanigan and moved to Miami. Flanigan served in the U.S. military and died while serving in Vietnam. She would later marry Alain Chovel and have a son. Her husband passed away shortly before Elly in 2007.

In Miami Chovel went on to become a real estate agent with EWM Realtors and Shelton and Stewart Realtors, her sales at one point put her in the top 1 percent nationwide. She developed a close friendship with Monsignor Bryan O. Walsh, the Miami priest who came from Ireland and was instrumental in developing Operation Pedro Pan. In 1991, Chovel founded the Operation Pedro Pan Group, allowing the adults who were part of the exodus to help preserve the historic record and contribute to Catholic Charities, the Archdiocese of Miami's humanitarian mission.

In 1998, Chovel joined a New York pilgrimage to witness Pope John Paul II's visit to Cuba. After Walsh died in 2001, Elly led an effort to realize his dream: to open a village for children in need. In 2006, the Monsignor Bryan O.

Walsh Boystown Children's Village, a shelter for children who were abused or in need, opened its doors. On November 2, 2012, a street sign on S.E. 15th Road and Brickell Bay Road in Miami was named in Elly Chovel's honor. I met Elly and participated with her in a couple of events in Miami. Although I did not know her well, I recall her friendly disposition and gentle character, she displayed a soothing presence. (Information for this article taken from *The Miami Herald* November 11th, 2012).

Santiago Ródriguez arrived at age 8 along with his younger brother and spent the next six years in an orphanage in New Orleans. His mother had concealed money along with a note begging the nuns at the orphanage to continue his musical education. Two years after his arrival, he made his concert debut at age 10 performing Mozart's Piano Concerto No. 27 with the New Orleans Philharmonic. In the artist's official website we learn that his international career was launched in 1981 when he won The Silver Medal at the Van Cliburn International Piano Competition; he also received a special prize for the best performance of Leonard Bernstein's "Touches", a work commissioned for the competition.

Just how good a pianist is Rodriguez? He has been called a "phenomenal pianist" (*The New York Times*) and "among the finest pianists in the world" (*The Baltimore Sun*). He has performed internationally with leading orchestras, including The London Symphony, the Dresden Staatskapelle, the Weimar Philharmonic, the Yomiuri-Nippon Symphony orchestra of Japan, among many others.

Mr. Rodriguez has appeared in recital at the Schauspielhaus in Berlin, Leipzig's Gewandhaus, Queen Elizabeth Hall in London, Montreal's Theater Maisonneuve, the Santander Festival in Spain, Alice Tully Hall in New York, The Kennedy Center in Washington, D.C., the Herbst Theater in San Francisco, the Ambassador Auditorium in Pasadena, and at the prestigious Ravenna Festival in Italy where the critics proclaimed that "he conquered the audience".

Santiago Rodriguez also enjoys a distinguished reputation as a teacher and master-clinician. Since 1980, he was a member of the Piano Division at the University of Maryland where he held the rank of Professor and Artist-in-residence. Beginning in September, 2009, he accepted the same positions at the Frost School of Music, University of Miami. He holds a Masters degree from the Julliard School, where he studied on full scholarship as a pupil of Adele Marcus, and he completed his undergraduate studies magna cum laude with William Rice at the University of Texas.

In August, 2012, the Florida International Piano Competition appointed Santiago as its new artistic director. With an ideal destination, a substantial purse, and the highest of standards, the FIPC has attracted prominent pianists from as far away as China and Australia (Information taken from *The Orlando Sentinel*).

An obituary note in *The Miami Herald* of February 18, 2011, discusses the life of Agustín De Rojas de La Portilla, who invented a type of extended wear contact lens and came to the United States during Operation Pedro Pan. He died of a massive heart attack in Palm Beach County at age 65.

De Rojas was the president of Quest Optical in Boca Raton, a company that holds several patents for lenses. For his many inventions, De Rojas was inducted into the Optical Pioneers Hall of Fame in 2008. But his life in America began at age 15 when he and his cousin, Ernie, were among the 14, 048 Cuban children sent alone to the United States by their parents who feared they would undergo communist indoctrination in Cuba under Fidel Castro's regime.

After arriving in Miami in February 1961, De Rojas and his cousin stayed briefly at what was called the Kendall camp, one of several locations where the Cuban children were housed until they could be relocated. He was eventually sent to the same St. Augustine school where former Florida Sen. Mel Martinez, and fellow Pedro Pan, also stayed. De Rojas was eventually reunited with his parents and went to live in Gorshen, N.Y. He married his high-school sweetheart, Regina, and until his death, the two were inseparable, relatives said.

After obtaining a degree from Columbia University, De Rojas became a chemist for the optical industry. He eventually moved to Palm Beach County and opened his company. He and his wife called the area home for the past 36 years.

Ángel B. Canete was born in Manzanillo and at age 9 had an experience that forever changed his life. He was riding his bicycle near a cemetery on the outskirts of town when he witnessed a Castro militia execute a group of men with a shot to the head and saw the bodies fall to the ground. This traumatic event caused Angel to stutter, an impediment that occasionally affects him to this day. After he told his parents, they decided to send him to the United States.

He arrived in Miami on January 14, 1962 and went to the Florida City Camp where he spent his first night there listening to children crying for their parents. Ten days later he was relocated to St. Vincent's Home, a Catholic orphanage in Saginaw, Michigan. Seven months later, his youngest sister arrived and was taken in by relatives in Miami. After she expressed a desire to be with him, Angel worked odd jobs until he had enough money to buy her a plane ticket. On August 1963, she arrived at the orphanage and brother and sister were reunited.

They stayed there for a couple of years until they were told that their parents had managed to flee Cuba and were on their way to Los Angeles. On December 23, 1965, a Michigan State Senator became aware of their plight; he helped cut the red tape, secured funds for the airline tickets, and his special assistant placed both Angel and his sister on a flight to Los Angeles. It was truly a wonderful, joyous Christmas family reunion. The Canete family settled in Van Nuys, California where his dad found a job picking up shopping carts at local stores' parking lots. His mom worked in factories and Angel held two jobs, delivering newspapers and working at a liquor store. Angel attended Los Angeles Valley College and graduated with honors with an Engineering Technology degree, specializing in Tool Design. The summer of 1972 was a turning point in his life; he married his sweetheart Poldy, he enrolled at the College of Engineering at California State University, Long Beach, and a month later was hired by Rockwell International, Space Division, Downey.

The Space Division facility in Downey was responsible for the manufacturing of the Space Shuttle's upper and lower forward fuselage, crew compartment, forward reaction control system and aft fuselage. He was assigned to the Shuttle's Crew Compartment Design Team, his expertise in tool design and advanced material manufacturing processes, made it possible to be part of this elite group of engineers.

In 1974, he graduated from California State University, cum laude, with a B.S. degree in Engineering Technology, and was immediately re-assigned by Rockwell to the Apollo Soyuz Docking Station Program. At the young age of 24, and with two years in an aerospace manufacturing environment under his belt, he was given his first engineering project management role.

The docking module vessel was formed from a welded cylinder of 1.58 cm thick aluminum, with a tapered bulkhead and tunnel section on the Apollo command module and a machined base assembly and bulkhead on the Soyuz end. His knowledge of manufacturing and welding techniques applicable to exotic aerospace materials, greatly contributed to the overall timely completion of the team's project. It is believed that Canete was the first Cuban-born and Pedro Pan engineer to have worked on both the Space Shuttle and Apollo Space Program. Today Angel is retired and lives with Poldy in Plantation Isles, Florida. They have three daughters and are expecting their fourth grandchild.

Armando Codina is Chairman and CEO of Codina Partners, LLC, a real estate investment and development firm based in Coral Gables, Florida. He formed Codina Partners in 2009 and through this entity and its affiliates is engaged in multiple real estate development and investment activities. The firm's portfolio includes mixed-used projects, commercial buildings and other investments primarily in Florida.

He arrived at age 14 in 1961 with a change of clothes, an old Cuban coin and not speaking a word of English. He was relocated to an orphanage in New Jersey where occasionally he was bullied and beaten by older boys. After three years in the orphanage and in and out of foster homes, Codina's mother finally arrived in the United States and he was reunited with her. He did not want his mother to work so he began to support both by working and, even though today he is a multimillionaire, he never achieved a college education.

His first job was bagging groceries at a Winn-Dixie grocery store; he also worked as a teller at a bank where he learned from some of his physician clients that medical billing systems were primitive and unwieldy. So Codina took out a loan of $60 thousand and started a company for computerized billing. Several years later he sold it for over $5 million.

As Chairman and CEO of Codina Group, the firm grew to be Florida's largest privately-held commercial real estate company. Before establishing Codina Group, he served as President of Professional Automated Services, Inc., a company created in 1970 to provide data processing services to physicians. As a result of the firm's success, Codina is recognized as a pioneer in the development of comprehensive medical management systems, including processing, accounts receivable, management reporting and multiple financial services.

In September of 2011, Codina received the Urban Land Institute's Lifetime Achievement Award. Other awards he has received over the past 15 years are: the University of Florida Bergstrom Center Hall of Fame Award; "Free Enterpriser of the Year" by the Florida Council on Economic Education; "Developer of the Year" by the National Association of Industrial and Office Properties (NAIOP); "Office Developer of the Year"; "Shopping Center Developer of the Year"; and "Entrepreneur of the Year" by the Wharton School.

In addition, he was honored with "Humanitarian of the Year" Award from the American Red Cross, "Sand in My Shoes" lifetime achievement award from the Greater Miami Chamber of Commerce; and the Merage Foundation's "National Leadership Award", which recognizes leaders whose journeys to the United States as immigrants have made a positive impact on the quality of life for all Americans. (Preceding information taken from ccresfl. com, voicesofchange.weebly.com).

Imagine a seven year old girl, frightened, and boarding a plane all by herself to a strange land. That's exactly the story of Rodri Rodríguez. She arrived and stayed for a short period at Florida City before being relocated to a foster home in Albuquerque, New Mexico. Rodri is President and CEO of Rodri Entertainment Inc., an international entertainment production company, founded in 1976. But Rodriguez's presence has been felt in the entertainment arena since 1975, when she played a key role in the decision to have the Latin category added to the Grammy Awards. In recognition of her efforts to give this music genre long overdue and deserved recognition, she accepted one of the first Grammys awarded in this new category for Mongo Santamaria.

One of the company's events is the Mariachi USA Festival heralded as the world's preeminent Mariachi festivals, which this coming year celebrates 20 years of sold out success at the Hollywood Bowl. Entrepreneur to the core, Rodriguez is amongst the group of 27 successful entrepreneurs that in 2006 became Founding Shareholders of the first Latino-owned bank in California in 35 years. Promerica Bank caters to the growing Latino entrepreneurship in the number one Latino market in the nation.

Rodri's international work has extended to Mexico, Argentina, Chile, Brazil, Israel and Europe and includes concerts/shows with Herbie Hancock, Stanley Clark, Andy Williams, Vikki Carr, Sammy Davis Jr., Julio Iglesias, Eric Clapton, Bryan Adams, Natalie Cole, Sara Vaughn and the creation and production of Playboy's Girls of Rock and Roll. Among the Latin artist concert productions are: Lola Beltran, Roberto Carlos, Raphael, Pedro Vargas, Vicente Fernandez, Armando Manzanero, Jose Jose, Gloria Estefan and the Miami Sound Machine, among a few.

In 2002, Rodriguez was elected to the Los Angeles County Fair Association, the first Latina elected to this Board. She is also the Founder and Chairman of the Mariachi Foundation which provides grants for Mariachi and Folklorico programs for K1-K12 in California, Texas, Arizona and Washington. On June 29, 2006, at the Writers Guild Theater in Beverly Hills, Rodri Rodriguez was honored as the National Latina Business Woman of the Year by the National Latina Business Women Association. On September of 2004 *Hispanic Magazine* selected Rodriguez to receive their Entertainment Award previously presented to Anthony Quinn and Gloria Estefan. (Preceding information taken from www.rodri.com).

Hugo Llorens came to the United States at the age of seven in April 1962 and stayed with an uncle in Miami, Florida. As of May 2012 he serves as the Assistant Chief of Mission in Kabul, Afghanistan. Prior to this assignment he was on the National War College faculty and served as Ambassador to Honduras from September 2008 to July 2011. Prior to his assignment as Ambassador, he served for 2 years as the Deputy Chief of Mission (DCM) at the American Embassy in Madrid, where he took up his duties on September 1, 2006. Ambassador Llorens was also Deputy Chief of Mission at the American Embassy in Buenos Aires, Argentina, where he served for three years from August 2003 until July 2006.

From 2002-2003, Hugo Llorens was Director of Andean Affairs at the NSC, where he was the principal advisor to the President and National Security Advisor on issues pertaining to Colombia, Venezuela, Bolivia, Peru and Ecuador. Prior to the NSC, he served for three years as Principal Officer at the Consulate General in Vancouver, Canada. In Vancouver, he created a novel multi-agency "Law Enforcement Hub" that included the opening of FBI, ATF, U.S. Customs, Secret Service, and Regional Security offices to work with Canadian counterparts on counterterrorism and international crime investigations.

Prior to Vancouver, he was Deputy Director of the Office of Economic Policy in the Bureau of Inter-American Affairs, where he helped launch the FTAA negotiations in 1998. As a 30 year veteran, he has served in Tegucigalpa, La Paz, Asuncion, San Salvador, and Manila. Prior to joining the Service, he was an Assistant Treasurer at the Chase Manhattan Bank in New York.

He received his Master of Science in National Security Studies, National War College in 1997; Master of Art in Economics, University of Kent at Canterbury, England in 1980; and Bachelor of Science in Foreign Service from Georgetown University in 1977.

Mr. Llorens has earned three Superior and six Meritorious Awards. He is a past recipient of the Cobb Award for excellence in the promotion of U.S. businesses, was runner-up for the Saltzman Award for distinguished performance in advancing U.S. international economic interests, and was nominated for the James Baker Award for superior performance by a DCM. He speaks English, Spanish, Tagalog, and some French. (Preceding information taken from Kabul.usembassy.gov).

Ana Mendieta was a performance artist, sculptor, and video artist who is best known for her "earth body" art work. She arrived at age 12 accompanied by her 14 year old sister and spent the first weeks in refugee camps before moving to several institutions and foster homes in Iowa. In 1966, Mendieta was reunited with her mother and younger brother, her father joined them in 1979, having spent 18 years in a Cuban political prison for his participation in the Bay of Pigs invasion.

Ms. Mendieta attended The University of Iowa where she earned a B.A., an M.A. in Painting and an M.F.A. in Intermedia under the instruction of acclaimed artist Hans Breder. Through the course of her career she created work in Cuba, Mexico, Italy, and the United States. Her work was generally autobiographical and focused on themes including feminism, violence, life, death, place and belonging. Mendieta often focused on a spiritual and physical connection with the Earth, most particularly in her "Silueta Series" (1973-1980). The series involved the artist creating female silhouettes in motion- in mud, sand and grass- with natural materials ranging from leaves and twigs to blood, and making body prints or painting her outline or silhouette onto a wall. In 1983 Mendieta was awarded the Rome Prize from The American Academy in Rome. While in residence in Rome, she began creating art "objects", including drawings and sculpture.

In 1979 Mendieta presented a solo exhibition of her photographs at A.I.R. Gallery in New York. The New Museum of Contemporary Art in New York hosted Mendieta's first survey exhibition in 1987. Since her death, Mendieta has been recognized with international solo museum retrospectives such as "Ana Mendieta", Art Institute of Chicago (2011); "Ana Mendieta in Context: Public and Private Work", De La Cruz Collection, Miami (2012). In 2004 the Hirschhorn Museum and Sculpture Garden in Washington, D.C., organized "Earth Body, Sculpture and Performance", a major retrospective that travelled to the Whitney Museum of America Art, New York, Des Moines Art Center, Iowa, and Miami Art Museum, Florida (2004).

Her work features in many public collections, including the Solomon R. Guggenheim Museum, New York, Metropolitan Museum of Art, New York, Whitney Museum of American Art, New York, Museum of Modern Art, New York, Art Institute of Chicago, Centre Pompidou, Paris, Musee d'Art Moderne et Contemporain, Geneva, and Tate Collection, London. In 2009 Mendieta was awarded a Lifetime Achievement Award by The Cintas Foundation.

The talented and respected artist died under strange circumstances. She died on September 8, 1985 in New York from a fall from her 34th floor apartment in Greenwich Village where she lived with her husband of eight months. Neighbors told the police that the couple argued violently just prior to her death. Her husband was tried and acquitted of the murder; no one knows if Mendieta's death was a possible accident or suicide.

As explained in her website, artist Elena Maza was born in Havana and came to the United States in 1961, living in New Mexico with a foster family for a year until her own family was able to leave. A resident of the Washington, D.C., area since then, she studied architecture at Catholic University, where she gained her first exposure to the local arts scene working with a group of students at Walter Hopps' Washington Gallery of Modern Art.

She started painting in 1970 while working as an architectural draftswoman and designer, and studied later at the Corcoran School of Art. Her paintings have been exhibited nationally in juried and invitational shows. She has received a number of awards, including an individual artist grant from the county in 1994, and has been the curator for art exhibitions locally and in Delaware, where Collage of Culture: Many Visions One Community received a Governor's award. Ms. Maza is a past President of the Women's Caucus for Art of Greater Washington, and of The Cuban American Cultural Society of Washington. The artist has also taught Taijiquan, a Chinese martial art.

Lorenzo Pablo Martínez holds a Master's degree in Piano Performance from the Manhattan School of Music and a Doctorate in Music Education from Teachers College, Columbia University in New York City. As a pianist, he has appeared in recitals and on radio and television. He is also a prolific composer; his music has been performed nationally and at international festivals. The television show *Captain Kangaroo* featured some of his works, and for *Group Soup,* a children's book published by Viking, he contributed the title song. In addition, a book of his children's songs, *The Circus*, was published by Clarus Music Ltd.

His story is a bit different as he arrived at 18, the maximum age allowed in Operation Pedro Pan, along with a younger brother of 15 while their parents and sisters, including his twin sister stayed behind. They arrived in April, 1962 and stayed at Camp Matecumbe in Florida until September. They were relocated to Kennewick, Washington and lived with an American family until he turned 19, the cut-off age for the program. Then he and his brother lived with a second family until Lorenzo went to Washington State University on a music scholarship and his brother stayed with the family. In 1965 his sisters left Cuba via Mexico and joined him in Pullman, Washington. A year later they were reunited with their parents.

During his senior year at Washington State University, he received a fellowship that paid for his tuition to continue his graduate degree there in exchange for teaching piano to non-music majors. A week before classes started, he decided to leave, so he turned down the fellowship and went to New York although he had no money and no idea what to do. He went to the Manhattan School of Music and although the term was already in progress, he was accepted as a student. Two years later he graduated with a Master's and started his musical career in New York teaching, performing and composing.

Lorenzo translated all twelve episodes of *The Second Voyage of the Mini* produced by Bank Street College of Education for PBS, and published his own children's story, *The Ballerina and the Peanut Butter and Jelly Sandwich*. He recently completed a memoir of his Pedro Pan experience that is awaiting publication; he's currently working on a series of bilingual stories for children and a Young Adult mystery novel.

He has played important roles in the not-for-profit arena, overseeing the development and communications/ marketing departments at a number of international organizations specializing in education, health, and the arts. He has represented those organizations at international conferences and has been a lecturer at several New York institutions such as New York University, the New School, York College of the City University of New York, and the 92nd Street Y. After living in New York City from 1967 until 2004, he moved to New Jersey while continuing to commute daily to Manhattan. Last year he moved to Houston, Texas to be closer to his twin sister. (Preceding information taken from lorenzo_martinez.com).

Ledy García-Eckstein arrived in Miami at age six and was reunited with her parents four months later. She is Acting Director of the Denver Office of Economic Development (OED) Division of Workforce Development. Previously, Ledy was Executive Director of the Metro Denver

Workforce Innovation in Regional Economic Development (WIRED) Initiative and Senior Policy Analyst for the Denver OED.

She also served for eight years with the administration of former Governor Roy Romer as Policy Advisor and Executive Director of the Colorado Workforce Coordinating Council. Ledy has also been a Community Planning and Development Representative for the U.S. Department of Housing and Urban Development and worked as Assistant Director for Business Services and Contracts in the City and County of Denver's Division of Workforce Development. Ledy was recently appointed to the board of the Colorado Community College and Occupational Education System. She is on the Latino Advisory Committee for *The Rocky Mountain News*, the Colorado Public Defender's Commission, and the board of the Insight Center for Community and Economic Development.

Ledy has a B.A. from the University of Iowa and a Masters degree in Government from the University of Virginia, and was a Fannie Mae Fellow at the Program for Senior Executives in State and Local Government at the John F. Kennedy School of Government at Harvard University.

Francisco F. Firmat arrived on July, 1961 at age 11 along with sisters Chary, 13, and Maria, 9. He was subsequently relocated to a Catholic orphanage in Denver, Colorado. Today he is Judge Firmat, for the Superior Court of Orange County in California. Firmat is the recipient of the prestigious "West" Award granted by The Orange County Bar Association in California. This is the highest honor awarded by the OCBA; the West Award is bestowed upon an outstanding attorney or judge who has made significant contributions to advance and elevate justice and law. He was presented this recognition on January 17, 2013 in Irvine, California.

Judge Firmat has a B.A. from California State University in Los Angeles and a Law degree from Western State University. *The California Bar Journal* in an article dated October 2008 notes that in recognition of his long-term commitment to improving access to justice, Firmat was the recipient of the 2008 Benjamin Aranda III Access to Justice Award, cosponsored by the State Bar Judicial Council and the California Judges Association.

Maria Teresa Vélez, Ph.D, is Associate Dean, University of Arizona, Graduate College in Tucson, Arizona. When she arrived she was sent to live in a foster home in Albuquerque, New Mexico. Dr. Velez is a clinical psychologist licensed in the State of Arizona. At the university she is responsible for Recruitment, Admissions, Enrollment and Management, and Under-represented students. She is PI of eight federal and foundation grants focusing on building a pipeline of under-represented graduates, and on providing financial, academic and cultural support to graduate students at the university. She is the faculty advisor for the Graduate and Professional Student Council and the Woman of Color student organization.

Dr. Velez graduated from the Wright Institute with a Doctorate in socio-clinical psychology. She first came to The University of Arizona as a postdoctoral fellow. Shortly thereafter she became the director of Counseling and Testing Services, helping lead the first UA efforts to diversify the student body.

In 1996, she became an associate dean in the Graduate College where she has led campus-wide efforts resulting in the doubling of minority graduate enrollment in 12 years. Currently 24% of graduate students at The University of Arizona identify as belonging to a minority group. Dr. Velez has created several pipeline building and graduate student recruitment and retention programs, garnering over 18 million dollars from the federal government and private foundations and obtaining an institutional commitment of over one million dollars every year from UA.

Dr. Velez has served on many national boards advancing diversity including the Council of Graduate Schools' Minority Advisory Board and the GRE Board's MGE Committee. She is also the recipient of many awards, the latest of which include the ACS Stanley C. Israel, Regional Award for Advancing Diversity in the Chemical Sciences, the UA's Vision Award, the UA's Peter W. Likins Inclusive Excellence Award and the 2008 UA Homecoming Alumni's Award.

Ricardo Viera is an artist specializing in painting, drawing, and engraving. He arrived on September 11, 1962 at age 17 along with a sister, Maria del Carmen, 11. They already had a 14 year old brother who arrived a couple of months ahead of them. He was living in a foster home for boys in Florida City Camp. His sister was placed there in an all girls residence with a family they knew well from Cuba. Ricardo was sent to nearby Camp Matecumbe. Fortunately for them their parents arrived one year later. In 1973 he studied in the School of the Museum of Fine Arts, Boston. In 1994 he graduated with a Master's of Fine

Arts (M.F.A.), from the Rhode Island School of Design, Providence. Between 1988 and 1989 he was the curator of the 24th Annual Contemporary American Art Exhibition. In 1989 he made the curatorship of the exhibition *William Rau*, Photographer: The Lehigh Valley Railroad Photographs.

In 1994 he worked also in American Voices: "Cuban American Photography in the USA"; in FotoFest'94, Fifth Biennial International Festival of Photography, Houston. In 1998 he was the curator of *Josef Bajus, Design Exploration Mixed Media*, in DuBois Gallery, Lehigh University Art Galleries. In 1979 he exhibited his works in "Ricardo Viera", in the Sardoni Art Gallery, Wilkes College, Pennsylvania. In 1985 he presented *Island on my mind* in the Museum of Contemporary Hispanic Art (MOCHA), in New York. In 1986 he made another personal exhibition: "Ricardo Viera: Computer Graphics 1986", in the Kemesen Museum, Bethlehem, Pa. In 1987 he presented his works *Ricardo Viera: Computer Art,*, in the East Stroudsburg University Art Gallery, East Stroudsburg, Pa.

Ricardo has participated in numerous collective exhibitions, among them in 1977 *Reencuentro cubano 1977,* Museo Cubano de Arte y Cultura, Miami. In 1982 he was one of the selected artists to conform *Young Hispanics U.S.A.*, in the 27th Annual Contemporary Art, Ralph Wilson Gallery, Lehigh University Galleries. Viera has won many awards, such as the Cintas Foundation Fellowship, New York City 1974-75. In 1980, 1981 and 1984, he was awarded the Pennsylvania Governor's Award for Excellence in the Arts. His works can be found as part of important collections, such as the Cintas Foundation, the Cleveland Museum, the Noyes Museum in New Jersey. Viera's art can also be seen in the Tel Aviv Museum, Tel Aviv, Israel.

Maria de los Angeles Hernandez Valero arrived in Miami at age 12 on February 17, 1962, accompanied by her 10 year old brother Nicolas Pablo. They stayed at the Florida City Camp until April 1962, when they were relocated to a foster home in Lake Charles, LA. A very kind American family, the Goodwin's, took care of them along with two of their own children. The foster parents requested to be called Tio and Tia (uncle and aunt) knowing that they could never replace Maria's parents.

On Maria's 13th birthday, 4 months after arriving in the United States, the Goodwin's took them on vacation to Disneyland and Hollywood. They lived with them for one year, then they were reunited with their parents and their younger sister Teresita Victoria in New Orleans.

There is a very interesting story about Maria's father and his encounter with Lee Harvey Oswald, the assassin of President John F. Kennedy. On August 8th, 1963, her dad went looking for employment in downtown New Orleans. When he got off the bus, he saw Oswald parading with a sign that read, "Fair Play for Cuba". Her dad became upset that someone in the United States would support a communist regime that forced him into exile. Since he was not fluent in English, he called a couple of Cuban friends who would act as interpreters in order for him to argue with Oswald. But instead of a verbal altercation, a fight broke out, the police intervened and everyone was arrested.

The following day the judge found Oswald guilty of disturbing the peace and fined him $25. Maria is adamant that the portrayal of the encounter of the Cubans with Oswald in the JFK movie by Oliver Stone was erroneously presented.

In 1974 Maria moved from New Orleans to Miami, where she worked at the Cuban Refugee Center until 1979 when she relocated to Boston. In 1981, she was awarded a scholarship at The New School for Social Research in New York City, where she lived until 1986. From there she moved to Houston to teach at the University of Houston- Clear Lake. In 1995, she received a doctoral degree in Public Health from The University of Texas, and after graduating was awarded a post-doctoral fellowship at The University of Texas MD Anderson Cancer Center.

During the past 15 years she has been a faculty member at MD Anderson, conducting health disparities research in the area of environmental health and childhood obesity among children of Mexican origin. In 2009, she was awarded the Fulbright Scholarship to conduct cancer prevention research at the Universidad Autonoma del Estado de Mexico in Toluca, where she is an invited professor.

Miguel R. San Juan was born in Havana and came to the U.S. in 1962 at the age of 11 along with a sister and they lived at the Florida City Camp. Then they were sent to a foster home in the state of Washington where they resided for several years before being reunited with their parents. Interestingly, when they landed in Miami they were placed under the custody of Catholic Charities. As noted in a news release by *Catholic Charities Atlanta* dated February 25, 2013, the same organization announced that San Juan has been appointed its new Chief Executive Officer. He has been active in public service at local, state, and federal levels. In 1990, President George H.W. Bush appointed him as the first national Export Council President.

San Juan recently moved to Atlanta from Houston, Texas where he served as managing Director of Global Invest Ventures and Capital, a business consulting firm. Prior to that role, he served as Senior Vice President for Business Development where he had a leadership role in a $32 million fundraising campaign known as Opportunity Houston. He helped build a campaign and program model which has allowed the Houston region to proactively market itself for jobs and investment.

Regarding his assignment as the new CEO of Catholic Charities, San Juan said the following, "I would like to do my part, as Pope John Paul II said, "to assure that the needs of the whole society are satisfied". Miguel plans to do this by focusing on four key areas: expanding current services, expanding strategic partnerships, increasing public awareness, and increasing fundraising avenues. San Juan lives in Roswell with his wife, Lucia Navarro. Lucia is an anchor on CNN Español's morning show Café CNN. He has three sons.

Dr. Raul Cano Chauvell was 16 when he came on February 17, 1962. He was relocated to Spokane, Washington where he attended Gonzaga University for one year and then served in the military. Upon his return he graduated from Eastern Washington University with a B.S. and a M.S. in Biology, specializing in Genetics. In 1974 he earned from the University of Montana a Ph.D. in Microbiology.

He then worked as an Assistant Professor at California Polytechnic State University, San Luis Obispo. After 35 years of academia, he retired and is currently an Emeritus

Professor of Microbiology. He has also founded an environmental consulting company. While at Cal Poly Dr. Cano was the founder and Director of the Environmental Biotechnology Institute (EBI). He raised $5.6 million to build new research facilities for the EBI and to establish new research programs. As founding Scientist of Ambergene Corporation, he directed the isolation and characterization of more than 1,200 ancient microorganisms from amber, including 9 ancient yeast, 4 of which are brewer's yeasts.

He is best known for his groundbreaking work in ancient DNA and microorganisms and his work has been published in scientific journals including *Science, Nature, Microbial Ecology, Applied and Environmental Microbiology*, and many more. Dr. Cano has received more than a dozen awards, including the prestigious Carski Award, written several textbooks and laboratory procedures manuals, has served as scientific consultant to several biotechnology firms, and has been elected fellow to the American Academy of Microbiology. He has been married for 44 years and has three children, all graduates from Cal Poly with degrees in Business, Nursing, and Biomedical Engineering, respectively.

Felipe de Jesus Estévez arrived in the United States at 15 in 1961. He was relocated along with 25 other Cuban boys to Fort Wayne, Indiana. There he completed his secondary education and pursued his dream of becoming a priest. He holds a Licentiate in Sacred Theology from Montreal University, a Master of Arts degree from Barry University and a Doctorate in Sacred Theology from the Pontifical Gregorian University in Rome. He is fluent in Spanish, English, French, and Italian.

He was ordained a priest in Fort Wayne in 1970. He was a member of the Canadian Society of Foreign Missions and was a missionary in Honduras until 1975. He was received into the Miami Archdiocese in 1975 and incardinated there in 1979. He was made a Prelate of Honor, with the title "Monsignor" in 1981, and named an Auxiliary Bishop of Miami in 2003. On June 1, 2011 Estevez was named Bishop of the Roman Catholic Diocese of St. Augustine in Florida. (Preceding information taken from America's Catholic Television Network).

Magali R. Jerez arrived on August 8, 1961 at 14 years of age. She has a Master of Arts in Language and Education from Montclair State University in 1976. She has been honored by Cambridge Who's Who for Excellence in Language Instruction. Magali is the Chairwoman of World Languages and Cultures Discipline for the Paramus, Hackensack and Lyndhurst Campuses of Bergen Community College in New Jersey.

Since taking over World Language and Cultures Discipline, Professor Jerez managed to expand the language program from 5 to 11 languages. Honored by Bergen Community College president G. Jeremiah Ryan for her contribution and selected for a Ph.D. scholarship by the U.S. Department of Education, she attributes her success to her diligence, determination and love for teaching languages. (The preceding information was taken from *Cambridge Who's Who*).

In a note in *Virginia Tech News* dated November 12, 2010, Antonio Fernández-Vázquez, associate professor of Foreign Languages and Literature in the College of Liberal Arts and Human Sciences at Virginia Tech, was conferred the "Associate Professor Emeritus" title by the Virginia Tech Board of Visitors. Antonio arrived on September 13, 1962 at age 13 and was relocated to a foster home in St. Petersburg, Florida. He recalls that he did not speak English and his foster parents not a word of Spanish. So how did they communicate? His guardians knew a married couple who spoke Italian so they would get together and Antonio would speak Spanish, the couple would then use their Italian to understand what he was saying, and interpret into English. Fortunately for Antonio he was reunited with his parents on March 1963.

A member of the Virginia Tech community since 1979, Fernandez-Vazquez made significant contributions to the understanding of Latin American studies through his work with Cuban exile literature. In addition, he supported the practice of proficiency-based assessment and instruction of foreign languages on a national level through the Interagency Language Roundtable Review Board and The American Council on the Teaching of Foreign Languages.

At Virginia Tech he taught a wide variety of courses ranging from first-year Spanish to graduate-level courses and received numerous teaching awards. He also directed the Intensive Summer Language Institute for 21 years. Fernandez-Vazquez received his Bachelor's degree from St. Andrews College and a Master's degree and Ph.D. from the University of Kentucky.

Lourdes Rodríguez-Nogues, ED.D., came to Miami on February 10, 1961, at age 13, with her brother Enrique who was 10. They stayed at the Kendall camp for about a month and then were relocated to Brooklyn, New York where they lived for just three weeks. Their final destination was Immaculate Heart of Mary Home for Children in Buffalo, New York. Then in October they relocated with their parents to Puerto Rico.

She received her degree in Counseling Psychology from Boston University in 1983. Lourdes wrote her thesis in graduate school on the psychological implications of premature separation in unaccompanied minors (Boston University, 1983). She has worked in the field of psychology in Boston for more than 20 years. Lourdes has had experience in community mental health, college counseling, and private practice. Some of her areas of interest and expertise are loss and grieving, trauma, depression, cultural identity, immigration and acculturation, life transitions, working with gay and lesbian individuals, and couples.

Dr. Rodriguez-Nogues has also worked as a consultant in the workplace, especially around issues of diversity, facilitating workshops and focus groups, and developing interventions and curriculum. She is a co-editor of the book *Out in the Workplace: The Pleasures and Perils of Coming Out on the Job.*

Lourdes Gil teaches in the Modern Languages Department as well as in the Department of Black and Hispanic Studies at Baruch College. She has a B.A. from Fordham University, and attended the Universidad Complutense de Madrid for her graduate studies. She holds an M.A. from New York University. She is primarily a poet and essayist.

Her poetry collection include *El cerco de las transfiguraciones, Empieza la ciudad, Blanca aldaba preludia, Vinculo el fuego de la especie* and *Neumas*. Her poems have been anthologized in *Burnt Sugar: A Cuban anthology,* edited by Oscar Hijuelos; *Las palabras son islas,* and published by Editoral Letras Cubanas in Havana.

Her essays on the art and literature of the Cuban Diaspora have been included in books, journals and encyclopedias. Among them, *Inventing America,* edited by Ruth Behar; *Remembering Cuba; Legacy of a Diaspora,* edited by Andrea O'Reilly Herrera; *Las relaciones culturales entre Estados Unidos y America Latina despues de la Guerra Fria,* edited by Ellen Spielmann and published by UNAM. Lourdes also participated in the historic "First Symposium of Writers from Inside and Outside Cuba", held in Stockholm in 1994, and her lecture was published in *Biopolaridad de la Cultura Cubana* by the Olof Palme International Center of Sweden.

Lourdes Gil has been the recipient of writing fellowships from The Ford Foundation, The Geraldine R. Dodge Foundation, The Poetry Society of America and the Oscar Cintas Foundation. Writers' residency fellowships include the Virginia Center for the Creative Arts, Vermont Studio Center, Casa de Andres Bello in Caracas, Venezuela, and the U.S. Japan Foundation.

Octavio Cisneros was 16 when he arrived on October 4, 1961. He was relocated to Marquette, Michigan where he attended high school. Octavio then studied at St. Lawrence Minor Seminary in Mount Calvary, Wisconsin, from where he obtained an Associate of Arts degree, and at Niagara University, earning a Bachelor's degree. He studied theology at DeSales School of Theology in Washington, D.C., and at Immaculate Conception Seminary in Huntington, New York, earning a Master's in Divinity. He was ordained to the priesthood by Bishop Francis Mugavero on May 29, 1971. Today Cisneros is Auxiliary Bishop of Brooklyn, New York.

For the first eight years of his priesthood, he served as parochial vicar at St. Michael's Church, Sunset Park in Brooklyn. In 1979 he was named diocesan coordinator of the Hispanic Apostolate and eight years later was appointed pastor of Our Lady of Sorrows Church in Corona, Queens, New York. His subsequent appointments were as an Episcopal Vicarate and as rector of Cathedral Seminary Residence in Douglaston. He was named a Prelate of Honor by Pope John Paul II in 1988.

Bishop Cisneros serves as vice-postulator of the Cause for Canonization of the Servant of God Felix Varela, a Cuban priest who served in New York for almost 30 years, ministering to Irish immigrants in the early part of the 19th century. The bishop is a founding member and president of the Felix Varela Foundation. (Preceding information taken from The Roman Catholic Diocese of Brooklyn).

Maria Cristina Halloran arrived on April 20, 1962 at age 11. She spent some time at a girls camp in Florida City (she celebrated her 12th birthday three days after arriving at the camp) until May 18th when she was relocated to Queen of Heaven Orphanage, Denver, Colorado. Maria Cristina was reunited with her parents in October 1963. Her mom and dad were scheduled to leave Cuba on October 1962 the day after President Kennedy declared a blockade of the island and flights were canceled. They were finally able to depart on a cargo ship that transported medicine to the island by the Red Cross. Her parents reunited with her in Denver and resided there until they passed away.

Maria is a full-time instructor and a Community College of Aurora (Colorado) faculty member since 1994. She teaches Grammar, Composition, Conversation, and Reading, ranging from the beginning to advanced levels, for the English as Second Language Department. She is also participating one class per semester in a cohort that aims to better link students to faculty in a more singular fashion and connect the classroom to the college's resources more efficiently.

Ms. Halloran also serves as Chair of Global Initiatives Committee. In addition to her CCA teaching resume, she has vast instructional experience at Metro State, Columbia College and Kent Denver, been a private interpreter and translator for the government and in the corporate world, and worked in banking. Her educational background includes a dual Masters degree from Denver's branch of Webster University in Human Relations and Management, with an additional Masters of Arts degree in Art History from the University of Madrid, Spain. She earned a triple major in Art History, Spanish and French from Colorado Women's College as an undergraduate.

Carlos Rubio Albet came to the United States on July 28, 1961 at 17 years of age and he stayed in Miami with friends of the family. He completed his high school education in Wilmington, Delaware. He has a B.A. in Foreign Languages from Concord College and a Masters of Art in Latin American Studies from West Virginia University. Rubio currently holds a teaching position at Shepherd University in Shepherdstown, West Virginia.

Rubio is a writer and his first short story was published while attending Concord College in Athens, W.V.

His work in English and Spanish, has appeared in the anthologies *20 Cuentistas Cubanos, Cuban American Writers, Distinct Voices, Narrativa y Libertad* and *Motu Proprio.* In 1989 his novel *Quadrivium* received the "Nuevo Leon International Prize for Novels". He has been twice a finalist in the Letras de Oro literary competition. In 2004 his novel *Dead Time* received Foreword Magazine's Book of the Year Award. His latest work is a novel entitled *Forgotten Objects.*

Luis Antonio Hernández, my brother, is an Early Childhood Education Specialist with TTAS-Western Kentucky University. (The following biographical data is from the National Center for Latino Child and Family Research). He is a Board member of National Latino Children's Institute, the only national Latino organization that focuses exclusively on children. NLCI's mission is to serve as the voice for young Latinos.

Luis holds a M.A. in Bilingual/Multicultural education from the University of San Francisco. He attained his undergraduate degree from Hampshire College, Amherst, Massachusetts where he serves on the Board of Trustees and leads the Student Life and Enrollment Committees. He is active in a number of national organizations that support children and family interests. At National Center for Latino Child and Family Research he is active in the new accreditation process, and developing professional and leadership development opportunities. He currently serves on the Board of the Parent Services Projects in California, the Advisory Board of the McCormick Tribune Center for Early Childhood Leadership, and the United Way's Center for Excellence in Early Childhood.

He has served on the Boards of the Florida Children's Forum, the Child Care Workforce, and NACCRRA, the Child Care Resource and Referral Agencies. A regular speaker at national, state, and local conferences, his special interests include early literacy, second language learning, collaboration and partnerships, changing demographics and diversity, adult learning, and ECE management topics. A few years ago he joined U.S. Secretary of Education Arne Duncan at the Annual Conference and Expo of The National Association for the Education of Young Children (NAEYC) to discuss the essential need for investment in education in the earliest years.

My brother is unaware that I am including him in this book. But I am certain that our parents, both of humble origin with a sixth-grade education, must be beaming with pride from heaven at what their first son has accomplished. *Mami* and *papi*, you taught us well and we honor the sacrifice you made for us.

Flora M. González Mandrin arrived on January 11, 1962, at 13 years old. She was educated in California and majored in Spanish with a minor in French at California State University at Northridge. In 1982 she received her Ph.D. in Hispanic Literature from Yale University.

She has taught at Emerson College in Boston as a Writing, Literature and Publishing (WLP) professor for the past twenty five years. Flora specializes in Latin American fiction and culture. She is writing a memoir about her experiences as a Cuban American, tentatively titled *On the Other Side of the Glass*, and has been anthologized in a number of publications. Her credits also include two nonfiction books, *Jose Donoso's House of Fiction: A Dramat-*

*ic Construction of Time and Place* (1995) and *Guarding Cultural Memory: Afro-Cuban Women in Literature and the Arts* (2006). Dr. Gonzalez has previously served as a fellow at the W.E. B. Du Bois Institute at Harvard University, and has taught at the University of Chicago, Middlebury College, and Darmouth College. (Preceding information from Emerson College).

Luis T. García Menendez arrived on April 20, 1962, when he was 12. He stayed briefly at Florida City before being relocated to the Mariana's Boys Home in Wichita, Kansas. Luis recently retired as a member of the Rutgers-Camden University (N.J.) faculty as a professor of Psychology. He served as Chair of the Department of Psychology for many years and also served as the Associate Dean of the Graduate School-Camden, stepping down on December 2011, after five years of service.

Under his leadership, the Graduate-School Camden grew exponentially, adding Master's degree programs such as Creative Writing and Computer Science. He also oversaw the implementation of the campus' first Ph.D. programs, in fields as varied as Childhood Studies, Computational and Integrative Biology, and Public Affairs. Dr. Garcia was also an outstanding instructor. Among other teaching awards such as the Alumni Association Outstanding Teaching Award and the Psi Chi Teacher of the Year Award, he received the prestigious Lindback Award in 2011, and he was honored with the Provost's Award for Teaching Excellence in 2005. His classes, in areas ranging from Psychology and the Law to Psychology of Human Sexuality, were always full, and students were often clamoring to conduct research with him.

Dr. Kenia Maria Casarreal passed away on April 20th, 2010 in Palm Beach, Florida after suffering with various illnesses for 10 years. She was born in Manzanillo, Cuba on January 3, 1946, and arrived as a Pedro Pan at 14 years old with her sister Ady. Her parents and brother came to the United States 18 months later.

She graduated from Marian College in Indianapolis, Indiana with a B.A. summa cum laude at only 19 years of age. Kenia married Leo Clouser in 1966 and had twins Leo and Kimberly in 1967. She then earned her M.A. and Ph.D. degrees in Organizational Psychology from Claremont Graduate School, Claremont, California. Kenia also earned additional M.A. degrees in Education (Special Education), Psychology and Education Psychology from California State University in Los Angeles, California.

Kenia divorced in 1976 and married Jake Adajian in 1984 and was his loving wife for 26 years. She had extensive national experience in a wide variety of non-profit and grassroots organizations such as Watts Community Center, Project Head Start as Parent Coordinator; Sophia Salvin Special Education Early Childhood Unit Model Project; and El Centro Mental Health Center. She also performed on a pro bono basis for innumerable consultations for grassroots AIDS, women's, minorities' and children's organizations. Kenia was named Arts Patron of the Year in 2005, she was a founding member of the Legacy Society of the Long Beach Museum of Art, past trustee of the LBA Collector's Circle and she and Jake had been long-time supporters of the Carpenter Performing Arts Center.

Dr. Casarreal was a board member subscriber and patron of the Long Beach Symphony Orchestra as well. Her legacy is to CSULB's College of the Arts to the "Dr. Kenia Casarreal-Adajian and Judge Jacob Adajian Scholarship Fund" for the promotion of voice, opera and College of the Arts. (Preceding information published in the *Long Beach Press-Telegram* from April 28th to April 30th, 2010).

Graciela M. Anrrich arrived on September 1, 1961, at the age of 13 along with a sister, 12. They spent a short time at Camp Kendall in Miami where they had a bitter-sweet experience: they missed their parents and younger sisters and would cry every day, especially around dinner time. But the camp had enough activities to keep them busy and occupied. Graciela recalls the excitement when Lissette Alvarez and her sister arrived at the girls' camp. They were the daughters of famed artists Olga Chorens and Tony Alvarez; Lissette's was the voice in the famous children's song *El Ratoncito Miguel,* which all Cuban youngsters knew by heart. After 3 weeks at the Kendall camp Graciela and her sister were sent to The House of Providence, an orphanage in Syracuse, New York, and were later placed in separate foster homes. Divine intervention at the hands of Graciela's foster family enabled the two sisters to live together in a warm, loving home. Graciela was able to be reunited with her parents and sisters 8 months later, in May 1962. So what became of Graciela? She is a faculty member in the ESL/Foreign Languages Department at Miami Dade College's InterAmerican campus. Some of the courses taught by Dr. Anrrich include Writing Level I, Advanced Grammar I & II, Accent Reduction I (Consonants) and Accent Reduction II (Vowels). She is affiliated with the College's Project ACE, the Accelerated Content-Based English. ACE is the accelerated English program for learners of English as a Second language. She has a B.A. in Mathematics and a M.A. in Linguistics, both from Florida International University, and a Ph.D. in Spanish Linguistics from Georgetown University. To this day she is grateful and thankful that her parents made the difficult decision to send her and her sibling to a land of freedom and opportunity.

Nicolas Sánchez arrived on December, 1960 at 15 years of age. Months later a brother and sister came also and he was reunited with his parents nine months later. Nicolas was a Professor of Economics at College of Holy Cross in Massachusetts for many years until he retired in 2010. In 1967 he obtained his Bachelor of Science in Economics (cum laude) from California State Polytechnic University in Pomona, California. He went on to complete a M.A. and a Ph.D., both in Economics, from the University of Southern California in 1969 and 1972, respectively. His first full time academic post was at Texas A&M University, where he taught, among other courses, Economic Growth and Development at the graduate level.

His publications have appeared in some of the top Economics journals in the United States and abroad, including *Cuadernos de Economia*, *Explorations in Economic History*, and *Journal of Economic Behavior*, to name a few. His field of specialization was property rights analysis, but his interest in Cuban affairs led him to publish articles and reviews for *Cuba in Transition*, *Cubans Studies*, *Journal of Comparative Economics*, and *South Eastern Latin Americanist*. In addition, he has published over one hundred articles and reviews in books, magazines, and newspapers.

Dr. Sanchez has also been a guest lecturer at Brandeis University, the University of Miami (FL), the Instituto Tecnologico Autonomo de Mexico, the Instituto Politecnico Nacional (both in Mexico City), the University of Valladolid (Spain), the University of Puerto Rico, Brown University, the University of Chicago, the University of Southern California and the University of Delaware. While at Holy Cross he taught courses for an interdisciplinary sequence, the First Year Program and the College Honors Program. He was also Chairperson of the Economics Department for three years and Chair of the Economics Honors Program for three years. (Preceding information from the College's web site).

José Azel left Cuba in 1961 as a 13 year old refugee. He holds undergraduate and graduate degrees in Business Administration and a Ph.D. in International Affairs from the University of Miami. He is currently a Senior Research Associate at the Institute for Cuban and Cuban-American Studies at the University of Miami. He is currently dedicated to the in-depth analyses of Cuba's economic, social, and political state, with a keen interest in post-Castro-Cuba strategies. Dr. Azel is author of *Mañana in Cuba: The Legacy of Castroism and Transitional Challenges for Cuba*, published in March 2010.

Dr. Azel was one of the founders of Pediatrix Medical Group, the nation's leading provider of pediatric specialty services and served as its Chief Financial Officer. He co-founded and serves as Board Chairman of Children's Center for Development and Behavior, an organization dedicated to providing therapies for children with autism and other pervasive developmental disorders. Dr. Azel was also an Adjunct Professor of International Business at the School of Business Administration, Department of Management, University of Miami. (Preceding information from cubanaffairsjournal.org)

Francisco J. Avellanet Garcia arrived with his sister on January, 1962 and was relocated to a foster home in Boston, MA. Today he is an inventor and Engineering Business Executive. He earned a Bachelor of Science in Mechanical Engineering and holds 27 patents as an inventor and has 3 pending applications. He has developed and commercialized dozens of life-saving medical devices, including a biologically-engineered stent which is suitable for multi-drug delivery and provides novel drug-eluting stents designed for improved performance over existing stents.

His many other invention involvements include an expandable endovascular support device (cited in *General Science and Technology*, March 2000), a guidewire for catheter, methods for making electrical cables having low electrical resistance, a polypectomy snare instrument (*GST*, January 2000), a surgical instrument with a rotatable shaft (*Scilogy*, March 2002), a high flexibility and heat dissipating coaxial cable (*GST*, October 2001), surgical basket devices, and many others.

Francisco "Frank"Angones Del Monte came to Miami on June, 1961 at age 10. He graduated magna cum laude from the University of Miami with a B.A. in 1972. He then obtained a Law degree from the University's School of Law in 1976. He is a member of the Executive Committee of the Florida Bar Board of Governors, was Past President (and first Latino) President of the Dade County Bar Association. He was also Past President (and youngest attorney) of the Cuban-American Bar Association. In addition, he was the first Cuban-born President of the Florida Bar (2007); the Florida Bar is the third largest State Bar in the United States.

He mainly focuses on Tort defense and commercial litigation in his Miami office. He is best known for human-rights cases, which include a 1994 case against the U.S. government for holding Cuban migrants picked up at sea at Guantanamo Bay and representing the families of those shot down in the Brothers to the Rescue mission in 1996. His great-great-grandfather was Pedro Figueredo, who was the author of the Cuban national anthem.

Cesar E. Calvet Lugones arrived on June, 1961 and spent time at camps in Orlando and Jacksonville, Florida. He holds a B.A. in Business Administration and Economics from Rollins College. He began his banking career as a teller in Sun Trust Bank in Central Florida in 1968. As of 2011 he coordinates the Latin Market and International Private Banking Services for Sun Trust Bank and serves on the Board of Hispanic Chamber of Commerce of Central Florida.

He has served as Chairman of Florida Housing's Board of Directors and Senior Vice President and General Manager of Grupo Bancario Latino for Sun Trust Bank, Central Florida. He has also served on several boards and commissions in the Orlando area, including the Metro Orlando Economic Development Commission, the Valencia Community College Foundation and the Metro Orlando International Affairs Commission.

Aldo de Jesus Martínez Paz spent time at Florida City Camp upon his arrival on February, 1962 and then was relocated to an orphanage in Totowa, New Jersey and a foster home. Today his career includes Law, Education and Investments. His undergraduate degree is from St. Peter's College (N.J.), and from Seton Hall Law School, Newark, New Jersey. He was Chairman of Intermarket Surveillance Group (ISG) from 2006-2007 and has participated in the ISG since 1989. He is a member of the College Board of Regents at St. Peter's College working with other Regents, faculty and administration on entrepreneurial initiatives. He is also a member of the Board of Directors at SMARTS Group Holdings.

He is also a Junior Achievement Board Member in New York and New Jersey. He represented the NYSE and worked with the Board to determine educational models to bring to the primary and secondary public and private schools and worked to identify curriculum and parent involvement opportunities. From 1987 to 2008 as a Junior Achievement Presenter, he provided in-classroom instructions on several courses including topics such as "Enterprise at Work" in primary schools and "International Markets" at the American High School of Economics & Finance (Church Street, Manhattan) 1987 to 2008.

At St. Ann School, Raritan, N.J., he was Vice President of the School Advisory Council March 2008 to 2010; President of the Council-providing, along with the other Council members, advisory function to the Principal and Pastor on all school matters including finances, curriculum and marketing. Aldo was the Recipient of the 1989 Humanitarian Award from "Jobs for Youths, Inc." of New York.

Hilarion Martínez Llanes arrived on March, 1962 at 7 along with his brother who was 8; they went to live with family friends. This highly educated Pedro Pan has a Bachelor's degree in Mathematics with Honors from Duke, a Law degree from the University of Florida, Master's in Law (in International and Comparative Law) with Honors from the University of Brussels, Belgium, and a Master's in Science in National Security Strategy from the National War College at the National Defense University. He was also awarded an honorary M.B.A. in Bilbao, Spain for having expanded U.S.-Basque commercial ties. He joined the State Department in 1986 and has served at U.S. embassies and consulates in Peru, Northern Ireland, London, Bilbao, Madrid, Florence and Greece.

During his career he has received numerous Superior Honor and Meritorious Honor Awards from the State Department. He has been a Visiting Professor in the Department of International Relations at Florida International University teaching a popular Diplomacy course. As of 2009 he is just one of 16 Senior Diplomats with the title of Diplomat in Residence. He was the first U.S. Consul to Bosnia and is fluent in Spanish, English, French, Italian and Greek. During his overseas assignments, he lectured at many of the U.S. universities study-abroad program and mentored American students interested in careers in diplomacy.

Octavio J. Visiedo was the superintendent of schools in Miami-Dade County, the country's fourth largest school districts, from 1990-1996. After six years he resigned and, in 1999, Visiedo became one of the four founders of Chancellor Academies, Inc., a leading developer and manager of high-quality, public charter schools and independent private schools serving students from pre-kindergarten through grade 12. Visiedo received both his B.A. in History and M.Ed. degrees from the University of Miami.

Mario Ernesto Sánchez is the Founder and Producing Artistic Director of Teatro Avante and the International Hispanic Theater Festival of Miami. He arrived in Miami on March, 1962 and then was sent to a foster home in New Jersey. He received the "Distinguished Career" award from the Florida Theater Conference for his contributions to the development of theater in South Florida. An accomplished actor, director, producer, and playwright, Mario Ernesto has worked in leading roles in several theater production and regularly works in film and television.

His productions have represented the United States at international theater festivals in Argentina, Brazil, Colombia, Costa Rica, Dominican Republic, Ecuador, France, Guatemala, Japan, Mexico, Portugal, Puerto Rico, Slovenia, Spain, Venezuela, Peru and in the United States (New York, Texas, New Mexico, North Carolina, and Los Angeles). He has also represented this country as a special guest at festivals and cultural events in several countries in Latin America and Europe. Mario Ernesto has served as a panelist in numerous arts boards at the local, state, regional, national, and international levels. He has worked in more than 40 films with major film stars. He also worked in Die Fledermaus, his first collaboration with the Florida Grand Opera. In 1994 he received the Ollantay Award, presented by CELCIT-Spain (Latin American Center for Creation and Research Theater), for his achievements on two continents.

In 1995, Mario Ernesto received the prestigious Federico Garcia Lorca award in Fuente Vaqueros, Spain, for his enormous contributions to the development of Hispanic Theater in America, and the Kusillo award, in La Paz, Bolivia for the same accomplishment. In 2007, he received the "Special Recognition Award" from the Arts and Business Council of Miami, to honor his contribution as the Producing Artistic Director of the International Hispanic Theater Festival of Miami, which he has been directing since its beginning in 1986. In October 2009, he received the FIT de Cadiz-Atahualpa del Cioppo Award in Cadiz, Spain, and in April 2012, the UCSUR Award in Lima, Peru. Mario Ernesto was appointed as Teatro Avante's representative to the Board of Directors of the Performing Arts Center Trust (PACT).

Antonio "Tony" Argiz arrived at age 8 and went to Mary Help of Christians, in Tampa, Florida. He is CEO and Managing Partner of Morrison, Brown, Argiz & Farra, LLP. MBAF is one of the top 50 accounting companies in the United States and the largest Florida-based in the state. In addition, *INSIDE Public Accounting* (formerly Bowman's Accounting Report), has honored MBAF for 13 years on its annual list of the nation's 25 best managed accounting firms. The company specializes in the areas of litigation, support, forensic accounting, business planning, valuation and audit services.

Argiz has a B.A. in Business Administration from Florida International University. He earned Leadership of the Year Award by the South Florida Banking Institute (2005), he is a member of FIU Foundation Board of Directors since 2006. He has also served in the governing body of the American Institute of Certified Public Accountants. He was the first Cuban appointed by the governor to chair Florida's Board of Accountability. He is a member of the Board of Trustees of the United Way of Miami-Dade County and has served as Vice-Chair of the Orange Bowl Committee. (Preceding information from foundation.fiu.edu).

Amarilys Gacio (now Rassler) came to the United States on August 28th, 1960 along with her sister Sonia and cousin Pete Gacio. Her mother arrived in December and her father on July, 1961. Amarilys and her sibling were taken in by a couple friend of the family. She originally lived in Miami but now makes Tampa, Florida her home. Amarilys graduated from the University of South Florida (Tampa) where she studied Spanish and Italian; in that same university she taught Italian as a graduate assistant. She wrote her first book, *Cuban-American, Dancing On The Hyphen*, in December 2011. The book celebrates her heritage and the blessings of living in the United States. Her literary work includes Cuban-American prose and poetry. The book reveals the author's yearning for her native land as well as her love and gratitude for her new home, the United States. Those who enjoy poetry and don't mind shedding a tear or two will definitely enjoy her book.

She has won awards for her Cuban-American poems such as "The Peanut Vendor" (El Manisero), "The Petals I Remember","In Memory of the Rafters", and "The Guava Newton". The author enjoys reading and dramatizing her poetry. She is currently working on a memoir, "Beyond The Veil", the story of her traumatic trip into the supernatural. Amarilys has an interesting personal life, she married her high school history teacher who later became an attorney. After 42 years of marriage she and her husband have a son, who graduated from Law school at 21 but then decided to become a teacher. Her daughter and son in law are both attorneys. Amarilys was a volunteer Industrial Chaplain for employees of Busch Gardens in Tampa for 15 years. She is very active in the Tampa Writer's Alliance and spends time with her grandchildren, and counsels those with emotional, mental and spiritual problems.

Maria Concepcion Bechily arrived at 12 years of age, was relocated to Chicago where social workers from Catholic Charities placed her in a foster home. She lived there until her parents were able to join her in the United States about a year and a half later. After college, she became a social worker for the very agency that had helped her, Catholic Charities.

Today Bechily is owner of Maria Bechily Public Relations, one of Chicago's first public relations firms dedicated to the Latino market. She is also a well-known philanthropist, from supporting arts education at the Goodman Theatre to co-chairing a campaign to raise millions to build the new Prentice Women's Hospital at Northwestern Memorial Hospital in Chicago. She is also a member of the Chicago Community Trust. She is an exceptional leader; for the Northwestern fundraising effort, the team that Bechily co-chaired surpassed the $150 million goal set for them, raising $207 million. Beginning in 2009 she was focused on her project Nuestro Futuro (Our Future), an effort at the Chicago Community Trust to help build Latino philanthropic efforts. (Preceding information from *Illinois Issues*, June 2009).

Lilia Tanakeyowma was almost 13 when she and her younger sister left Cuba. Lilia and her family were ultimately reunited and, after living in Florida and Michigan during the first two years in the United States, they relocated to California, where Lilia graduated from Foothill High School in Tustin. She credits her attentive and persistent high school teachers for not only helping her attain a proficient command of the English language, but also guiding her toward college.

She entered UC Irvine as a freshman in 1968 and graduated three years later with a B.A. in Spanish Literature and a job as an elementary bilingual teacher in the Santa Ana Unified School District (SAUSD). In addition to her educational service in Santa Ana, Lilia created time to contribute her talents in other locations: (1) teaching under Madeline Hunter at University Elementary School in the UCLA campus; (2) directing an Educational Talent Search Program at CSU, Fullerton: (3) serving as Executive Director for the Orange County Coalition for Immigrant Rights, a project of the Orange County Human Relations Commission; and, (4) serving as an Executive Assistant for the Fourth Supervisory District in Orange County.

Lilia earned her Ed.D. and her dissertation , *Student Engagement Among Immigrant and Non-Immigrant Youth: Mexican Descent Youth in a California High School*, explored the experiences of 31 tenth-grade students in one of SAUSD's largest comprehensive high- schools. The focus of her research stemmed from her experience both as an immigrant teenager herself and as a young teacher in Santa Ana of a mainly immigrant population, as well as from her passion to discover the socio-cultural factors that help Latinos succeed in school.

For more than a decade, Dr. Tanakeyowma has been an administrator at Santa Ana College. She currently serves as the Dean of Student Affairs at Santa Ana College, the community college that is the higher education destination for the majority of the graduates of the district in which she began her career thirty-eight years ago. Dr. Tanakeyowma's three daughters are proud that their mother serves as an example of what immigrants can achieve in this country. Like her, they've pursued higher education, and all have professional careers in fields that feed their own passion. (Preceding information taken from www.gse.uci.edu).

The Reverend Dr. Luis León, of St. John's Episcopal Church in Washington, D.C., was chosen to offer the benediction on January 21, 2013, at President Barack Obama's inaugural ceremony. Leon gave the invocation at President George W. Bush's inaugural in 2005. The church has been nicknamed the "church of the presidents" because it has had every president since James Madison attend its services, though not all have been members.

Luis Leon was baptized into the Episcopal Church in Guantanamo, Cuba. In 1961 he came to the United States as part of Operation Pedro Pan. He attended the University of the South, graduating in 1971. He received a Master's degree in Divinity from the Virginia Theological Seminary in 1977 and in 1999 was awarded an honorary Doctor of Divinity from the University of the South. The Reverend Dr. Leon is fourteenth Rector of St. John's Church, he began his tenure at St. John's in 1995. His specialty is building inner city parishes through spiritual leadership, preaching excellence in worship and liturgical music, stewardship and outreach that involves parish members in the community. Luis teaches courses nationwide in parish building and stewardship and is a frequently requested commencement speaker.

Before his time at St. John's, Luis served as Rector of Trinity Church in Wilmington, Delaware, and at St. Paul's Church in Patterson, New Jersey. St. Paul's, an urban parish, grew during his tenure from 35 parishioners to several hundred. In 1985 St. Paul's was named "Church of the Year" by the New Jersey Council of Churches, and in 1986 Luis was awarded the Bishop's Outstanding Service Award in recognition of the "extraordinary contribution made to the life, quality, and the spirit of the church in this diocese (Newark)". (Preceding information taken from www.st.johns-d.c.org).

Eduardo C. Robreno is a federal judge for the United States District Court for the Eastern District of Pennsylvania. He joined the court in 1992 after being nominated by President George W. Bush. Robreno was the first Latino federal judge in Philadelphia and first Cuban-American to become a federal judge in the United States.

He was born in Havana in 1945 and received his B.A. in Westfield State College in 1967. He then achieved a M.A. at the University of Massachusetts in 1969 and a J.D. in 1978 at Rutgers Law School. Robreno arrived as a 15 year old refugee who washed dishes to earn money to live, "with little more than a dream of a better life". His father, Eduardo, couldn't practice law when Fidel Castro came to power in Cuba. So he and his wife urged their son to flee Havana in 1961. Ingrained with his parents' values of freedom and education, Robreno embraced his opportunities-the Christian Brothers who educated him and the two foster families who cared for him in Florida and Massachusetts.

A graduate of Rutgers Law School, Robreno supervised his law firm's pro bono work, sat on the board of the Concilio, a Hispanic social service agency, oversaw a multi-family housing project for the elderly as an Episcopal Hospital board member, served as legal counsel for the Spanish Merchants Association and on the American Red Cross board.

When he was sworn in, Robreno thanked "Ramon" who "spent years in Cuban prisons for smuggling out visas for youngsters like myself to live in freedom". He was surely referring to Ramon "Mongo" Grau Alsina, who spent 20 years in prison for his role in Operation Pedro Pan. Polita Grau, Ramon's sister, served 14 years for the same offense. I met Mongo Grau in Miami and he was a very gentle, simple man who did not harbor any resentment or hatred toward his captors. He was the nephew of Ramon Grau San Martin, an ex-president of Cuba.

Pedro E. García was 15 when he and his younger brother arrived on August 6, 1962. They lived at Camp Matecumbe for a few months until their mother came; in 1963 his father arrived via Spain and the family relocated to Clorinda, Iowa. His parents are included in this book for their inspiring background and impact on the lives of their sons. Both were well educated even though they took different paths to completing their education. His mother, after completing her Bachelor's degree from the University of Havana, went to the United States and eventually earned two Ph.D. degrees. The first was from Fordham

University (this author studied there from 1971-1972) in New York City in Philosophy. The second was from the University of Texas in Spanish Literature. The importance of this achievement was that she received these advanced degrees before 1942, when most Latinas did not achieve such high levels of education.

His father, although very intelligent and talented, had dropped out of high school and went to work at his father's printing plant and newspaper. Once he met Pedro's mother and fell in love with her, they agreed that he had to return to school. I must add that the power of love makes a man melt before a lady! Eventually he earned university graduate degrees in Chemistry and Physics. His parents had been early supporters of the Castro revolution but grew disenchanted as the regime became totalitarian and communist. In June of 1961 Pedro's father was arrested by the secret police and held incommunicado for ten weeks. He was then blindfolded and placed in front of a firing squad and on command the soldiers shot over his head. They just wanted to intimidate him, a scene that was played out all too often after Castro assumed power. The day after his release Pedro's parents decided to leave Cuba.

After the family reunited in Miami, his mother was offered a job teaching Spanish in Clarinda, Iowa, a small community of 5,200 people. Her job was half-time at the community college and half-time at the high school. She was hired for two reasons: (a) she had an education, and (b) she spoke English. His father took a job as a custodian at the high school Pedro attended.

Today Dr. Pedro E. Garcia is a professor of Clinical Education at the Rossier School of Education at the University of Southern California. He is also working to develop an executive program for superintendents throughout the country. Once implemented, the vision of this institute is to provide a place for superintendents where they can collaborate, create working networks, finds solutions to common problems, influence national educational policies, develop international educational partnerships and serve as a center for advocacy for K-12 education. Dr. Garcia has been instrumental in the development of an on-line Master's level program for K-12 principals.

Prior to coming to USC in 2008, he served as superintendent of schools for 17 years. His last appointment was in Nashville, Tennessee from 2001-2008. At the time of his arrival in Nashville the high school graduation rate was 55%. In 2008, when he left Metro Schools the graduation rate had climbed to 79%. Dr. Garcia was the co-founder of the Nashville Alliance for Public Education which raised over 16 million dollars for public schools. He was instrumental in raising funds to build 15 new schools, modernize 35 other schools and build a state of the art staff development center. Dr. Garcia also served in California as Superintendent of the Corona-Norco Unified School District, (1994- 2001) and Superintendent of the Carpinteria USD from 1991- 1994. At the time he arrived in Corona the district's student achievement ranked 14th in Riverside County. When he left Corona the district was third in the County.

In 2003, President Bush appointed him to the National Presidential Commission on Volunteerism and Community Service. In 2002, while serving as superintendent in Nashville, he created an office for community engagement. In 2005, he opened the first Customer Service Center to help parents navigate the educational system. He also founded Alignment Nashville, which successfully created partnerships between the 134 Nashville public schools and over 500 non-profit organizations.

Dr. Garcia was honored as Nashvillian of the Year in 2003. Twice he has been a finalist for National Superintendent of the Year. In 2007, The Franklin Covey Inc. recognized him with their National Leadership Award. He also received the Apollo Award from the Public Relations Society of America. He has received four "Who's Who" nominations and the Outstanding Young Man of America Award. He was selected by the California School Library Association to receive their annual Administrative Leadership Award in 1996. He began his teaching career in 1971 in San Diego County. Dr. Garcia became the youngest high school principal in Los Angeles County in 1978 at the age of 31.

An avowed Christian, Dr, Garcia and his wife, Dr. Priscilla L. Partridge de Garcia, have five grown children and thirteen grandchildren. He earned his B.A. from Kansas University; his Master's from San Diego State University, and his Ph.D. from The University of Southern California. He enjoys many interests and hobbies, including going to the movies, photography, and listening to jazz. He plays the congas, sings, and has performed on the stage at the Grand Ole Opry, and Cheekwood in Nashville, TN. Who would have thought that a *cubanito* would one day play at the Grand Ole Opry?

Auto racing giant Ralph Sanchez passed away in Miami in April, 2013. The well-known businessman and Pedro Pan member, as noted in an article in *The Miami Herald*, made it possible for legendary drivers Mario Andretti, Emerson Fittipaldi and A.J. Foyt to race exotic cars along Biscayne Boulevard in downtown Miami.

As reported in the daily, IndyCar champions Michael Andretti, Al Unser Jr. and Danny Sullivan steered to victories on a road circuit laid out in Tamiami Park because of Ralph Sanchez. Jimmie Johnson has secured each of his five Sprint Cup Championships at a Homestead-Miami Speedway facility envisioned, planned, founded and brought to vibrant life by Ralph Sanchez.

Derek Bell, the British sports car ace who shared a 1985 Grand Prix of Miami victory with Al Holbert, said Sanchez "stood 10 feet (taller) than anybody else promoting things in those days.

"Miami set the bar for street races. Ralph created that ambiance and atmosphere. The Miami Grand Prix was an international event, and it boosted Miami's image worldwide".

Sanchez gave up a lucrative real estate development business to invest his money, his business acumen and his boundless passion into the 1983 inaugural Grand Prix of Miami on a demanding street circuit through Bayfront Park and along Biscayne Boulevard. Monsoon-like storms the morning of that 1983 inaugural flooded portions of the course and forced a scheduled 168-lap race to be halted after only 27 laps.

International Motor Sports Association sanctioning officials left up to the devastated Sanchez how much of the purse to distribute. Sanchez told them to pay the entire posted prize money. That gave him instant credibility, established his reputation in the industry and paved the path to all he achieved from then until the International Speedway Corporation bought out his interest in the Homestead-Miami Speedway operations partnership in the late 1990s. (Preceding information taken from miamiherald.com).

Mario Goico left Cuba in 1961 and was relocated to Mariana Children's Home, an orphanage in Wichita, Kansas, which provided for his care and education until he turned 18. He supported himself and paid his way at Wichita State University to earn a B.S. in Aeronautical Engineering and a Master's in Business Administration.

He was elected in 2002 to the Kansas House of Representatives. He has served in the following committees: Chairman of the Joint House and Senate Kansas Security; Chairman of the Military, Veterans and Homeland Security; Vice Chairman of Elections; Member of Taxation; Member of Federal and State Member of Financial; Member of Insurance; member of Local Government.

Goico retired from the Air Force Reserve as a colonel in 2002. He served for 32 years in the Air Force, Air Force National Guard, and Air Force Reserve. He is a "Desert Storm" veteran, having flown 36 missions; and a command pilot with more than 6,000 military flying hours. He worked at Boeing Aircraft Company from 1974 to 2005, having worked as a manager, marketer, engineer, and a pilot in flight test. He has received numerous community, military, and leadership awards including: The Air Force Legion Merit, Leadership Wichita, and The Outstanding Liaison Officer for the Nation. (Preceding information taken from mariogoico.com).

# Science/Academia

José Szapocznik, Ph.D., is a Havana native clinical psychologist of Polish-Cuban ancestry and one of the nation's leading family therapists specializing in Hispanic families. He is the developer of One Person Family Therapy and Brief Structural Therapy. He is director of the Center for Family Studies at the University of Miami, where he was inducted into its Iron Arrow Honor Society.

Dr. Szapocznik earned his B.S., M.S. and Ph.D. degrees from the University of Miami. He is Professor and Chair, Department of Epidemiology and Public Health; Associate Dean for Translational Research and Community Development; Director, Center for Family Studies at the University of Miami. According to his curriculum vitae, his primary research focus has been family therapy with drug abusing and problem behavior minority youth. He and his colleagues at the Center for Family Studies have conducted theoretical and empirical work testing some of the basic assumptions of family therapy, developing Brief Strategic Family Therapy and a number of culturally-specific variations of this approach, extending strategic structural family therapy techniques to overcoming the problem of engaging hard-to-reach families, and investigating the underlying mechanisms of action in Brief Strategic Family Therapy.

A second focus is a study of different methods of delivering HIV testing and counseling in drug abuse treatment service agencies. A third area of interest is his development of a major interdisciplinary program of research on the relationship between the built environment and psychological functioning and physical health. This work has focused on aspects of the built environment that affect school age Hispanic children's behavioral adjustment, the psychological and physical adjustment of Hispanic elders, and most recently, the risks to weight gain inherent in immigration. The latter includes studies of the pathophysiology of weight gain and the mechanisms through which gain in adiposity bring about progress toward metabolic syndrome. (Preceding information taken from szapocznik.pdf).

On February 11, 2011, *The Miami Herald* carried an obituary column about Matías G. Vega Pelegrino, Ph.D., (1924- 2011) Emeritus Professor of Modern Languages at Xavier University. He passed away at the age of 86 after a lengthy illness.

Dr. Vega was born in Santiago de Cuba, the son of a pioneer in Cuban radio. He attended the University of Havana where he was awarded a Doctorate in Social Sciences and Public Law in 1948, and subsequently received a Certificate in French Language and Civilization from the University of Paris.

After teaching in Cuba, Dr. Vega came to Xavier in 1954 and taught Spanish and French language and literature for 40 years, serving for years as the Chairman of the Department of Modern Languages. A dedicated and popular teacher and innovator, he was instrumental in the development of Xavier's language laboratory and established study programs abroad for Xavier students. Notably, Dr. Vega organized a student exchange program with the Universidad Javeriana in the Republic of Colombia.

In recognition of his achievements, Dr. Vega served as Grand Marshall at Xavier's Commencement in 1994. The Matias G.Vega Spanish Award is awarded annually to the Xavier University senior who demonstrates the highest linguistic achievement in Spanish and interest in Hispanic culture. After retirement, Dr. Vega cultivated lifelong interests in music and literature. He was also a past president of the Panamerican Society of Cincinnati.

Trauma Surgeon Dr. Juan A. Asencio is a Havana native; he immigrated to Chicago at the age of thirteen. He completed his undergraduate education with a double major at the University of Illinois. He earned his medical degree from Rush Medical College at Rush University and his surgical residency at Northwestern University in Chicago. Dr. Asencio completed his fellowship in trauma surgery and surgical critical care at the University of Texas Health Sciences Center Southwestern Medical School-Parkland Memorial Hospital in Dallas. His specialty is surgery and his sub-specialties are trauma surgery and surgical critical care. He is double board certified in surgery and surgical critical care and is a Fellow of the American College of Surgeons.

Dr. Asencio is both a nationally and an internationally recognized expert in the field of trauma surgery. His area of focused study and expertise is surgical techniques and outcomes for difficult injuries and difficult problems in trauma surgery. As an author, he has a total of 476 publications including peer-reviewed articles, book chapters and 15 books including 4 issues of the Surgical Clinics of North America and one issue of the Emergency Medicine Clinics of North America. He has lectured extensively nationally and internationally in Europe, North, Central and South America, Asia, Australia and New Zealand.

His social conscience led him to be involved in, and concerned with, the impact of violence in youth, particularly among Hispanic youth. He frequently addresses audiences nationally and internationally regarding urban violence and education. In October 2012 he joined Westchester Medical Center of Westchester, New York, as Chief of Trauma Surgery and Critical Care. (Preceding information taken from mypressmanager.com).

Miami-born Mireya Mayor, Ph.D., is a television favorite among wildlife enthusiasts. She is a scientist, explorer, wildlife correspondent, anthropologist, inspirational speaker, wife and mom. She has reported on wildlife and habitat issues to worldwide audiences for more than a decade. The only daughter of Cuban immigrants, she is a former NFL cheerleader for the Miami Dolphins. She eventually became the first female wildlife correspondent for the "Ultimate Explorer" series on National Geographic television and has spent years exploring some of the wildest and most remote places on earth.

As a child Mireya had birds, fish, dogs, cats, parrots, rabbits, turtles, and a little chicken named Maggie. But it was in 1996, while attending the University of Miami that she realized that her passion for animals could become a career. She took an anthropology course, not entirely knowing what that meant. She was fascinated by the class, particularly her professor's stories of chasing monkeys in the wild. She applied for a grant, was approved and went on to spend a summer in the remote jungles of Guyana, one of the most unexplored regions of the world at that time.

The following year she journeyed to the wilds of Madagascar into areas so isolated, that she often found herself surrounded by local villagers whom had never seen a foreigner before her arrival. Against all odds, and following in the footsteps of renowned scientists who had tried and failed, Mireya completed the first ever long-term and genetic studies of two of the most critically endangered primates in the world, Perrier's sifaka and the Silky sifaka. National Geographic offered Mireya the opportunity of a lifetime and her dream job: a staff wildlife correspondent position, complete with her own office. She has since gone underwater with six-foot Humboldt squids, scoped out gorillas in Central Africa, swam with great white and six-gilled sharks, and worked with leopards in Namibia (just to name a few projects).

In 2005, Mireya received two Emmy Award nominations for her work on the television series "Ultimate Explorer". She was later named an "Emerging Explorer" in 2007 by National Geographic which selects rising talents, "the next generation of visionaries" who push the boundaries of adventure and global problem-solving, inspiring people to care about the planet. She also starred in the Expedition Africa: Stanley & Livingstone (History Channel) as one of four explorers to retrace the nearly

1,000 mile trip of Henry Stanley and David Livingstone. Mireya is now one of the hosts on National Geographic's new channel Wild!. She is a Fullbright scholar, National Science Foundation Fellow and published author with a Ph.D.in Anthropology from Stony Brook University. (The information in this article is from Ms. Mayor's web site).

On June 1, 1996, the University of Miami recognized Dr. Agustin Castellanos, professor of medicine, for "33 years of devotion, distinguished work, and faithful service". Dr. Castellanos would remain on the faculty for another 15 years, amassing additional awards for his remarkable cardiology research and patient care, garnering more national and international recognition for the University through his published material and participation in dozens of conferences and scientific seminars, and instructing cardiology fellows, a task he described as "most fulfilling".

Dr. Castellanos, who died in Miami on December 7th, 2000, was a remarkable physician. He was a pediatrician, radiologist and cardiologist who was a pioneer in the filed of angiocardiography. His initial work was with dogs and cadavers before extending this method to humans. He and some colleagues published the first important paper on the clinical application of intravenous angiocardiography which was published in the *Archivos de la Sociedad de Emidios Clinicos* in 1937. This is believed to be the first publication which dealt with the normal cardiac structure and the changes seen in ventricular septal defect and pulmonic stenosis (Development of Angiography and Cardiovascular Catheterization, Dolby, T. 1976).

Dr. Castellanos was recognized in Cuba with the establishment at the Children's Hospital in Havana of the Agustin W. Castellanos Foundation for Cardiovascular Research. Internationally he was been honored in Mexico City by being included in the mural honoring the "Great Men of Cardiology" located in the Instituto Nacional de Cardiologia by the famous Mexican artist Diego Rivera. Dr. Castellanos was nominated for the Nobel Prize twice, in 1959 and 1960. Ecuador and Colombia nominated him for the Nobel Prize in Medicine and Physiology, respectively. After leaving Cuba for political reasons, in 1967 he passed the examination by the Florida Board of Medical Examiners and restarted his private practice again. He was 65 years old, an age when most physicians seek retirement.

His early research, conducted in Havana from about 1957 until his immigration to the United States in 1960, included studies of the normal vectorcardiogram in infants, a technical paper on vectorcardiography with resistance compensation using the Frank method, and left ventricular hypertrophy in the presence of left bundle branch block. After arriving in the U.S., Dr. Castellanos completed an internship at University of Miami/Jackson Memorial Medical Center, then joined the faculty as an instructor in medicine in 1962. He rose through the ranks while racking up wide recognition for clinical cardiovascular research focusing on electrocardiography and cardiac electrophysiology. He is the co-developer of the "Demand" pacemaker, now known as VVI pacemaker, and was the first to make a presentation on the device at national and international meetings. He also co-developed the AV sequential pacemaker, initially known as the "Bifocal" pacemaker, and co-directed the "Master Approach to Cardiovascular Problems" conferences, held annually for 31 years.

Among the different academic and institutional positions held by Dr. Castellanos include: Visiting (and later Clinical) Professor of Pediatrics at the University of Miami School of Medicine, Senior Scientist at the National Children's Cardiac Hospital, acting Chief of Pediatric Cardiology at Variety Children's Hospital (now Miami Children's Hospital), and Professor of Pediatrics at the federally sponsored International School of Medicine's Postgraduate courses for Foreign Medical Graduates (ECFMG). The 1925 graduate from the University of Havana School of Medicine and descendant of Central Asian and Mexican immigrants died at age 98 in Miami. (Preceding information from med.miami.edu/news and Finlay-online.com).

Ada Maria Isasi-Diaz (March 22, 1943- May 13, 2012) was professor emeritus of Ethics and Theology at Drew University in Madison, New Jersey. As a Hispanic theologian, she was an innovator of Hispanic theology in general and specifically of "Mujerista Theology". She was founder and co-director of the Hispanic Institute of Theology at Drew University.

She was born and raised in Havana to a Roman Catholic family. She graduated from Merici Academy in 1960 and arrived in the United States as a political refugee later than same year. She entered the order of St. Ursula (she left the order in 1969 before taking her final vows and became involved in the Women's Ordination Conference) and earned a B.A. from The College of New Rochelle in New York. In 1967 she went to Lima, Peru as a missionary for three years. Upon returning to the U.S. in 1969, she taught high-school in Louisiana; then lived in Spain for 16 months before returning to the United States. She continued her education, earning a M.A. in Medieval History from SUNY Brockport. Isasi-Diaz then achieved both a Master's of Divinity and a Ph.D. with a concentration in Christian Ethics in 1990 from Union Theological Seminary in New York City. In 2006, she was awarded a Doctor of Divinity honoris causa from Colgate University.

Her studies and involvement in the feminist theological movement led her to begin to develop a theology from the perspective of Latinas in the U.S., which led to the development of Mujerista Theology. This theology included their religious experiences, practices, and responses to the daily struggles of life. Early in her career Ada was very involved in the Women's Ordination movement within the Catholic Church. Isasi-Diaz was on the faculty of the Theological and Graduate Schools of Drew University from 1991 until her retirement in 2009. She was a panelist and occasional contributor to the "On Faith" on-line discussions at the Washington Post and Newsweek.

In 2007, she became an unofficial church pastor after the Archdiocese of New York closed Our Lady of Angels Catholic Church in East Harlem, the parish church she attended while in seminary. A group of parishioners began holding protests and prayer meetings outside the building, but eventually it became a neighborhood institution in which Isasi-Diaz was a leader where she delivered sermons. In March 2012, her invitation as a keynote speaker at Christian Brothers University was cancelled due to her support for the ordination of women to the Catholic priesthood and because she ministered at her nephew's same-sex marriage ceremony at a Unitarian Church in Washington in 2009.

Ernest Sosa is a philosopher specializing in epistemology, the brand of philosophy concerned with the nature and scope of knowledge. He is Board of Governors, Professor of Philosophy at Rutgers University in New Jersey. He has been at Rutgers full time since January 2007; previously he was at Brown University since 1964. He is one of the leading contemporary epistemologists, and has also written on metaphysics, modern philosophy and philosophy of mind.

He was born in Cardenas, Cuba in 1940. Sosa earned his B.A. and M.A. from the University of Miami and his Doctorate from the University of Pittsburgh in 1964. In his books *Knowledge in Perspective* (1991), and *A Virtue Epistemology* (2007), Sosa defends a form of virtue epistemology called "virtue perspectivism", which distinguishes animal knowledge from reflective knowledge.

Sosa is a past president of the American Philosophical Association and a fellow of the American Academy of Arts and Sciences. He edits the philosophical journals *Nous* and *Philosophy and Phenomenological Research*. In 2005, he delivered the John Locke Lectures at Oxford, which formed the basis of his 2007 book. He was also the 2010 recipient of the Nicholas Rescher Prize for contribution to systematic philosophy, conferred by the University of Pittsburgh biennially. Also in 2010 he was awarded the Quinn Prize by the American Philosophical Association. His son, David Sosa, is a professor and chair of the philosophy department at the University of Texas, Austin.

Cristina Fernández-Valle pertains to a growing group of women scientists. The Cuban-American has devoted her life to the study of neurovegetative diseases that mainly affect young people as well as to being a mentor for minority students who want to become scientists. Dr. Fernandez-Valle is the first minority scientist to join the faculty of the University of Central Florida's Burnett School of Biomedical Sciences, where she has spent 15 years guiding the career of hundreds of aspiring physicians and researchers.

The Latina investigator has received the National Role Model Award from Minority Access, an organization that seeks to improve diversity in education, employment and research nationwide. She is currently trying to discover the causes of neurofibromatosis Type Two, a disease, she said, "that attacks the peripheral nerves and grows very slowly and then becomes evident when the young people are between 15 and 19, when they begin to lose their hearing and their balance, something terrible for a child who is in the prime of life, running, studying for a career". (This information is taken from Fox News Latino).

Manuel (Manny) González was nine years old in 1961 when he and his parents fled Cuba. And fled is an understatement. They had been detained at the Havana airport by Cuban government agents and it appeared that their dream of living in liberty had vanished. But Che Guevara's plane landed and the guards rushed to greet their hero; then Manny's father hustled him and his mother to a waiting Pan American plane. But the agents soon followed the taxing plane and ordered that they be handed over. The captain explained that the plane was American property and the revolutionaries would have to deal with the U.S. government. So off went the Gonzalez family to a new life in Miami.

Manny attended Coral Park High School and then Miami Dade Community College (now Miami Dade College). His passion involved studying science, technology, math and engineering. But he also was interested in a military career so he applied to West Point. It took him three attempts before he was accepted. After four years of academic study and physical training, Manny Gonzalez became the first Cuban refugee to graduate from West Point.

Following his West Point graduation, he spent six years on Army active duty; then when Exxon offered him a job as a drilling engineer, he accepted and moved to Texas. In 1992, he and two friends formed their own company, Isotag (later renamed Authentix) which made brand-name protection molecular tags that could be placed in liquids-everything from perfume to liquor to gasoline and oil-to determine if the product is authentic or counterfeit.

That led, after another six years, to a job with Texaco's technology organization. In 2001, Texaco merged with Chevron, and Gonzalez has, since then, worked for Chevron, as manager of the Chevron Alliance with the Los Alamos National Laboratory. In 2012 Chevron nominated him for the HENAAC (Hispanic Engineer National Achievement Award Conference) Lifetime Achievement Award from the Great Minds in STEM organization.

What has Manny achieved during his tenure at Chevron? He has been granted 18 U.S. and international patents. He has published 16 professional papers; his appearance as a "world class authority" in articles by *The Wall*

*Street Journal*, CNN worldwide, *Business Week* and other publications. He was also awarded in 2012 for Excellence in Technology Consortium. His selection, along with his partners, by *R&D Magazine* for having developed "one of the 100 most significant technological advances introduced into the marketplace in 2011". Manny also won The Chairman's Award given by the CEO of Chevron for outstanding achievements. It was the first time in company history it was given to an individual instead of a group. (This information taken from latino.foxnews.com).

Eduardo D. Rodríguez, M.D., D.D.S., is Professor of Surgery, Chief, Plastic Surgery, at R. Adams Cowley Shock Trauma Center at University of Maryland Medical Center. His medical degree is from the Medical College of Virginia/Virginia Commonwealth University; his D.D.S. is from New York University College of Dentistry. His fellowships were at Johns Hopkins Hospital/University of Maryland Medical Center, Plastic Surgery; International Fellowship in Reconstructive Microsurgery, Chang Gung Memorial Hospital, Taipei, Taiwan. Dr. Rodriguez is Certified in Plastic Surgery; Oral and Maxillofacial Surgery.

In 2012 Dr. Rodriguez led a team of 150 doctors, nurses, and others at the University of Maryland Shock Trauma Center in the most extensive face transplant surgery ever performed in the world. The patient, Richard Lee Norris, received new skin and muscle and a new jaw, teeth and tongue to replace damage from an accidental gunshot wound he suffered 15 years ago. Mr. Norris had been living largely as a recluse since then, and the surgery gave him a new face and a new life. The operation took a total of 36 hours to complete. Previously in 2006, Rodriguez treated soldiers wounded by explosives in Afghanistan and Iraq. The techniques the Cuban-American physician and his team pioneered will help others, as will their efforts to reduce the side effects of anti-rejection drugs transplant patients must take for the rest of their lives. (Information for this article taken from latino.foxnews.com and baltimoresun.com).

Dr. Joseph Lámelas is Director of Minimally Invasive Heart Surgery, Cardiothoracic Surgical Associates in Miami, Florida. He is a board-certified cardiac and thoracic surgeon with many years of experience. Recognized as a leading authority in cardiovascular and thoracic surgery, Dr. Lamelas has performed more than 8,000 open-heart procedures. He is involved in training surgeons across the United States and South America in advanced and innovative surgical techniques. He has also participated in international operative surgical symposia, as well as lectured nationally and internationally.

He completed his training in cardiovascular and thoracic surgery at the State University of New York, Health Science Center of New York in 1990. He has published numerous articles and presented extensively on cardiac surgery. He is past President of the Cuban Surgical Society (U.S.-based 1999-2002), a council member of the Florida Society of Thoracic and Cardiovascular Surgery, a member of the Society of Thoracic Surgeons, and America College of Surgeons. He has consistently had one of the lowest morbidities and mortalities in the state of Florida. He is the senior partner in his private practice group, "Lamelas and Associates". The group operates/practices at 5 Miami area hospitals- Baptist Hospital of Miami, Mercy Hospital of Miami, Kendall Regional Medical Center, South Miami Hospital and Cedars Medical Center of Miami. (Preceding information taken from www.orlive.com).

Isabel Pérez Farfante (1916- 2009) was a Cuban-born carcinologist, or someone who studies crustaceans. She was the first Cuban woman to receive a Ph.D. from an Ivy League school. She returned to Cuba from the United States only to be blacklisted by the Castro government. Perez Farfante and her family escaped Cuba and she became one of the world's foremost zoologist studying prawns. She discovered large populations of shrimp off the coast of Cuba and published along with Brian Kensley one of the most noted books on shrimps: "Penaeoid and Sergestoid Shrimps and Prawns of the World. Keys and Diagnoses for the Families and Genera".

So how did this brilliant scientist get started? She completed her Bachelor of Science in 1938 from the University of Havana. After graduation she worked as an associate professor at the university. She married economist and geographer Gerardo Canet Alvarez in 1941 and then she was awarded a Guggenheim Fellowship in 1942 for biology and ecology. This award, along with an Alexander Agassiz Fellowship in oceanography and zoology, and a Fellowship at the Woods Hole Oceanographic Institution, helped support her education at Radcliffe College. She then received her Master's in Biology in 1944. This feat made her one of the first women to attend Harvard University. She then went on to get her Ph.D. from Radcliffe.

During this time she met Thomas Barbour in Washington, D.C. Perez Farfante was struggling to garner support for her projects in her department, and Barbour advised she work at Harvard. Barbour helped her get work there, and from 1946 until 1948 she was Associate Curator of the Museum of Comparative Zoology at Harvard. In 1948 she earned her Ph.D from Radcliffe, making her the first Cuban woman to obtain a Doctorate from an Ivy League institution. After graduation, she returned to Cuba and continued her career.

Upon her return, Perez Farfante served as full professor at the University of Havana until 1960. She also served as a shrimp researcher and then the director of the Cuban Fisheries Research Center until 1960, while still working as a professor. During this time, she and her husband Gerardo Canet welcomed the new government in the island. But she began having conflicts with the newly appointed co-director of the Research Center. Also during this time, it was requested that her husband accompany Che Guevara on trips abroad. Canet declined, wanting to be close to his wife and two sons. This led to the couple's inclusion on the Cuban government's blacklist. They sent their sons to the U.S. and a month later the two fled Cuba, leaving behind all their personal items, except for one suitcase.

Perez Farfante, with her family, returned to Cambridge, Massachusetts, and she found work back at the Museum of Comparative Zoology. There she served as associate in invertebrate zoology from 1961 until 1969. For a number of years she did independent research, receiving funding from Radcliffe College and the National Science Foundation. She began working as systematic zoologist at the National Marine Fisheries Service Lab at the National Museum of Natural History in Washington, D.C.

She researched the systematics of Penaeid shrimp. However, in her early work, in the late 1930s and 1940s, she studied Foraminiferans and mollusks. In the 1940s, while working at the Museum of Comparative Zoology, Dr. Perez Farfante worked with Henry Bryant Bigelow on his research about lancelets. By 1950 she had started focusing on commercial shrimp. She discovered large shrimp populations in the Gulf of Batabano and Isla de la Juventud, both in Cuba.

After escaping to the U.S., she focused on the Penaeid shrimp, specifically on reproductive morphology. She researched shrimp from shrimp farms in America on behalf of the U.S. Fish and Wildlife Service from 1961 to 1962. In her later years, while assisting at the Rosenstiel School of Marine and Atmosheric Science in Miami, she co-wrote a paper about Sergestoidea and Penaeidae shrimp in the Tongue of the Ocean.

Dr. Albert Siu is a general internist, geriatrician, and health services and policy researcher. He is currently a Senior Associate Editor of Health Services Research, a member of the U.S. Preventive Services Task Force and a director of the Visiting Nurse Service of New York. He is also Professor and Chair Geriatrics and Palliative Medicine, Professor Health Evidence and Policy, and Professor Medicine, General Internal Medicine. He is the Ellen and Howard C. Katz Chairman's Chair of the Brookdale Department of Geriatrics and Palliative Medicine at Mount Sinai Medical Center in New York City.

Siu was born in Havana of Chinese Cuban descent. He graduated with honors from the University of California at Berkeley with a degree in Biochemistry in 1976. He earned his medical degree from Yale University School of Medicine in 1986. After completing his residency in Internal Medicine at UCLA, he remained at UCLA as Associate Professor of Medicine, with a joint appointment as Health Services Researcher for the RAND Corporation in Santa Monica, where he was the author of 20 monographs.

He served as Chief of the Division of Geriatric Medicine at UCLA from 1989 until 1993, when he accepted a position as a Deputy Commissioner with the New York State Department of Health. Concurrently, from 1994 to 1995, Siu was Associate Professor of Health Policy and Management at the University of Albany School of Public Health. In 1995 he was named Professor in the Department of Health Policy. Dr. Siu is the author of 9 book chapters and more than 100 peer-reviewed publications. He has co-authored 50 publications for the U.S. Preventive Service Task Force. His department at Mount Sinai treats nearly 5,000 elderly patients a year and houses a number of signature programs including the Martha Stewart Center for Living, the Hertszberg Palliative Care Institute, the National Palliative Care Research Center, the Medicare Innovations Collaborative and the Mount Sinai Visiting Doctor.

Ysrael Abraham Seinuk (1931-2010) was a structural engineer who designed the structure for many landmark skyscrapers in New York and around the world. He also taught structural engineering at New York City's Cooper Union and was ranked by *Time* magazine as one of the 25 "Most Influential Hispanics in America". Seinuk was born in Havana in 1931, the only child of immigrant Lithuanian Jews. Ysrael graduated from the University of Havana in 1954 and fled Cuba to New York after the communist revolution. Seinuk recalled that he arrived in the United States with little more than $20 in his pocket, "my slide ruler and my diploma from the University of Havana".

In New York he joined the engineering firm of Abrams, Hertzberg & Cantor. He later became a partner of what became known as Cantor Seinuk. He also founded a separate firm, Ysrael A. Seinuk, P.C. in 1977. Seinuk became one of the world's foremost experts in the structural design of skyscrapers. *The New York Times* wrote that he "made it possible for many of New York City's tallest new buildings to withstand wind, gravity and even earthquakes". He has been credited with innovations in the use of reinforced concrete as a structural material in skyscrapers. Elizabeth O'Donnell, associate dean of architecture at Cooper Union, called Seinuk "the person who brought reinforced concrete to New York City, because this was primarily a city where its high-rises were structured in steel". In 2004, *Real Estate Weekly* wrote, "you can't walk down the streets of Manhattan without seeing a building that famed structural engineer Ysrael Seinuk hasn't touched".

Seinuk and his company engineered more than 50 high-rise office buildings and hundreds of apartment structures in New York. He was dubbed "Mr. New York" for his engineering of New York's skyscrapers. Seinuk worked on a number of skyscrapers for Donald Trump, including the 70-story Trump World Tower, Trump International Hotel and Tower, and the 58-story Trump Tower on Fifth Avenue. Trump said of Seinuk, "Ysrael Seinuk and his staff are the best in the business".

Other structures that Seinuk worked on include New York's Lipstick Building, the New York Mercantile Exchange, the 48-story Conde Mast Building, the 45-story Bear Stearns Building, and the Arthur Ashe Stadium. He also worked on the Chapultepec Tower in Mexico City and the 0-14 Tower in Dubai. Seinuk was honored with The Fazlur Khan Lifetime Achievement Medal from the Council on Tall Buildings and Urban Habitat in 2010. He was also a licensed engineer in 15 states, the District of Columbia, Puerto Rico, and the United Kingdom.

John Henry Silva was born in Chicago, Illinois in 1980. He is an author, entrepreneur, and military veteran. His grandfather was a friend of Ernest Hemingway and his cousin, Al Montoya, is the first Cuban American player in the National Hockey League. Silva graduated from New Trier High School and Harvard University. He enlisted as a U..S. Marine rifleman and served on Yankee White duty at The White House during the administrations of Bill Clinton and George W. Bush. He served in over 25 domestic and international trips supporting Presidential Travel Operations. He is a recipient of the Presidential Service Badge. Silva also served in Washington, D.C. during 9/11 and was deployed for Operation Iraqi Freedom.

Silva is a serial entrepreneur, and serves as a Partner at Otsuki Consulting International, a private firm that funds and provides management consulting services for clients operating in East Asia and North America. Previously he was a co-founder of Quorum PR, Planetary Emissions Management, and Boston Life International School. He also served as a consultant for Aga Khan University in Karachi and Zedaka Foundation in Moscow. He has published academic research at iRobot and Harvard Business School, and founded the online media platform Tech Politique. He was also an editor for *Humanism and Business,* published by Cambridge University Press. Silva has been a Researcher at Harvard Business School and Teaching Fellow at Harvard Kennedy School of Government, and currently he serves as a Visiting Researcher at Harvard University.

Carmen M. Reinhart (nee Castellanos) arrived at age 11 with her family in 1966. She is the Minos A. Zombanakis Professor of the International Financial System at Harvard Kennedy School. Previously, she was The Dennis Weatherstone Senior Fellow at the Peterson Institute for International Economics and Professor of Economics and Director of the Center for International Economics at the University of Maryland.

She is a Research Associate at the National Bureau of Economic Research, a Research Fellow at the Center for Economic Policy Research, Founding Contributor of Vox-EU, and a member of Council on Foreign Relations. She is also member of America Economic Association, Latin American and Caribbean Economic Association, and Association for the Study of the Cuban Economy.

Dr. Reinhart graduated from Florida International University in 1975 with a B.A. in Economics (summa cum laude) and then earned her Ph.D. at Columbia University. Professor Reinhart held positions as Chief Economist and Vice President at the investment bank Bear Stearns in the 1980s. In the 1990s, she held several positions in the International Monetary Fund. From 2001 to 2003, she held the position of Deputy Director at the Research Department at the International Monetary Fund. She has been the Minos A. Zombanakis Professor of the International Financial

System at Harvard Kennedy School since 2012. She has served on the editorial boards of *The American Economic Review*, the *Journal of International Economics*, *International Journal of Central Banking*, among others. In both 2011 and 2012 she was included in the *50 Most Influential* ranking of *Bloomberg Market* Magazine.

Her work has helped to inform the understanding of financial crises for over a decade. Her numerous papers on macroeconomics, international finance, and trade have been published in leading scholarly journals. She is coauthor of *A Decade of Debt* (2011) and *Assessing Financial Vulnerability: An Early Warning System for Emerging Markets* (2000). Her best-selling book (with Kenneth S. Rogoff) entitled *This Time is Different: Eight Centuries of Financial Folly* (2009), which has been translated into 20 languages, documents the striking similarities of the recurring booms and busts that have characterized financial history. The book won the 2010 TIIA-CREF Paul Samuelson Award and the Gold Medal in the Council on Foreign Relations Arthur Ross Book 2011 Awards.

Dr. Luis Fernández III is Chairman of Trauma and Surgical Critical Care at Trinity Mother Frances Hospital in Tyler (Texas) and Brigadier General of the Texas State Guard Medical Brigade. He arrived with his family at age seven escaping political persecution and a death threat against his father. As a youth in Cuba, Dr. Fernandez remembered that his father, also a physician, spoke out against injustice, including that perpetrated by dictator General Fulgencio Batista and later Fidel Castro.

The young Fernandez accompanied his father as he traveled to care for the sick and for Castro's wounded rebels. After Castro's regime had taken power, a former wounded rebel he cared for years earlier showed up at Fernandez's door to inform the doctor that because Fernandez would not head a medical department (much like the U.S. Surgeon General) under the Castro regime, he had been put on a "death list". Appreciative for Fernandez saving his life, the now-senior security chief told the doctor to take his family and flee. They left all their belongings behind and it was the last day the Fernandezes saw their native country.

Luis Fernandez III (his grandfather was also a physician) completed pre-medical studies at the University of Miami and received his medical degree from Mexico's Universidad Autonoma de Guadalajara, considered "Latin America's Harvard". He completed postgraduate training at Loyola University Stritch School of Medicine and the University of Illinois. Pathway and Surgical/Critical Care, including Subspecialty Rotation in Urology/Urologic Trauma Internships were completed at Resurrection Hospital in Chicago. Dr. Fernandez is Board certified by the American Academy of Experts in Traumatic Stress, American Board of Surgery in Surgical Critical Care, American Academy of Experts in Traumatic Stress and Forensic Traumatology.

During his fifteen plus years at Tyler's Trinity Mother Frances Hospital, he has been directly involved in caring for over 10,000 trauma patients whose lives were in danger. Dr. Fernandez is the recipient of numerous awards, including the William J. Vynaled, M.D. Award, Outstanding Resident in Surgery, American Medical Association of Physicians Awards for 1989, 1991, 1994, and 1997, and awards from the American Academy of Family Physicians from 1994-1996, and the Captain William Barron Chapter, Sons of the American Revolution, Emergency Medical Services Commendation Medal. Dr. Fernandez's academic positions include: Clinical Assistant of Surgery and Family Practice at the University of Texas Health Center at Tyler, Adjunct Professor of Nursing and Medicare and Physician Preceptor at the University of Texas at Arlington and Clinical Professor of Surgery at the University of Chicago Pritzken School of Medicine.

Following the 9/11 attacks in New York City, he joined the Texas State Medical Brigade. As Commanding Officer, he was instrumental in ensuring that evacuees of hurricanes Katrina, Rita, Gustav, and Ike received excellent medical care in special needs shelters manned by State Guard soldiers. His achievements have been recognized by the Governor of the State of Texas and the Texas State Guard Adjuvant General, and Dr. Fernandez's accomplishments were further acknowledged with his promotion to Brigadier General of the Texas State Guard Medical Brigade.

He was also the recipient of the Medals and Ribbons of the Texas Military Forces, two Texas Outstanding Service Medals, three Adjuvant General's Individual Awards, two Commanding General's Individual Awards, and two Humanitarian Service Ribbons. He also won the Association of Military Surgeons of the United States Medal, Commissioner Officer Association Ribbon, State Guard Association of the U.S. Ribbon, and Texas State Guard Ribbon. On March 10th, 2010, Dr. Fernandez was selected as the Texas State Winner of the Daughters of the American Revolution

Americanism Medal. (Preceding information taken from www.tmfhs.org).

Dr. Nohema Fernández is Dean of the Claire Trevor School of the Arts and a Professor of Music at the University of California at Irvine. The Department of Music's profile of Ms. Fernandez notes the following: "As a pianist, Nohema Fernandez performs worldwide as recitalist and symphony soloist. The Cuban-born pianist formally debuted in Havana at age 16. She has recorded for the Musical Heritage Society, Protone Records, Music Masters, and Centaur Records, and is the recipient of the NEA Solo Recitalist Fellowship for performances of Pan-American works and the Distinction of Honor "La Rosa Blanca" (Los Angeles) for her support of Cuban music and culture. Her articles have been published in Piano Quarterly and Latino American Music Preview, and she is the editor of "Toward the End of the Century: Cross-Cultural Minority Perspective", published by The College Music Society".

Prior to joining UC Irvine in 2001 as Associate Dean, she was the Interim Head of the Media Arts Department and Professor of Music (Piano) in the College of Fine Arts at The University of Arizona. From 1995 to 1997 she served as President of the College Music Society, a non-profit organization that gathers and disseminates ideas on the philosophy and practice of music as an integral part of higher education, addressing interdisciplinary issues within music, and examining broader educational concerns. She also served as Chair of the Society's Committee on Cultural Diversity. Ms. Fernandez has a Doctorate of Musical Art from Stanford University. (Preceding information taken from music.arts.uci.edu/Fernandez).

Cuban-born Virgil Suárez is a Professor in the English Department at Florida State University. He specializes in creative writing (fiction and poetry) and Latino/a (especially Cuban-American) literature. He is a poet, essayist, novelist and short story writer. He earned a M.F.A. from Louisiana State University in 1987. Suarez is the author or co-author of over fifteen books of poetry and prose. His work has appeared in *The Kenyon Review, The Southern Review, The New England Review, Poetry London, Poetry Wales, Poetry New Zealand, Imago* (Australia), *The Toronto Review* (Canada), *The Barcelona Review* (Spain), *Ploughshares,* and many others nationally and internationally.

Professor Suarez is the recipient of the following accolades:

Best America Poetry, 2004

G. MacCarthur Poetry Prize, 2002

The Daily News/The Caribbean Writer/University of The Virgin Islands Poetry Prize, 2002

National Endowment of the Arts Fellowship, 2001

The Book Expo America/Latino Literature Hall of Fame Poetry Prize for Best Book of Poetry (for *Banyan*), 2001

Winner of a Florida State Individual Artist Grant, 1998

Winner of New York Public Library's Best Book for the Teenager, 1993

Nominated to five Pushcart Prizes

He has also reviewed books for *The Los Angeles Times, The Miami Herald, The Philadelphia Inquirer,* and *The Tallahassee Democrat.*

Alejandro Portes, Ph.D., is a premier sociologist who has shaped the study of immigration and urbanization for 30 years. He is Chair, of the Department of Sociology, at Princeton University as well as co-founder and director of Princeton's Center for Migration and Development. In 1998, Portes became a Fellow of the American Academy of Arts and Sciences, and he was elected to the National Academy of Science in 2001. From 1998 to 1999, Portes served as president of the American Sociological Association. He has authored and edited numerous books and has published articles on a range of policy issues, including immigrant assimilation, Latin American politics, and United States/Cuba relations.

Portes began his under-graduate studies at the University of Havana in 1959 but left after one year due to the turmoil of the Cuban Revolution. He left because he opposed the communist regime and became a political exile. He continued his education in Argentina and eventually completed his B.A. in Sociology in 1965 at Creighton University in Nebraska. He began his doctoral studies at the University of Wisconsin in Madison, which housed one of the strongest sociology departments in the country. In addition to the Ph.D. that he earned in 1970, the University of Wisconsin later awarded Portes an honorary doctorate in 1998. In 2001, Portes's alma mater further distinguished him by asking him to deliver the inaugural William H. Sewell Memorial Lecture.

While Portes centered his early work on first-generation immigrants, he later expanded his research to include the children of these immigrants who were growing up in the United States. His study showed that first-generation immigrants may return to their country of origin, but their U.S.-born children are U.S. citizens with American aspirations, and most are here to stay.

In the late 1980s, Portes and his colleague Ruben G. Rumbaut (also profiled in this book) launched a labor-intensive project called the Children of Immigrants Longitudinal Study (CILS). The goal of the study was to find out what happened to these children as they grew up in an environment divided between American society and their parents' culture. The key concept that came out of CILS was that of "segmented assimilation", integration into different segments of American society rather than into one mainstream community. In 2001, Portes published the results of CILS in *Legacies: the Story of the Immigrant Second Generation*, co-authored with Ruben Rumbaut. The book has won several awards, including the Distinguished Scholarly Publication Award from the American Sociological Association. (Preceding information taken from www. pnas.org Biography of Alejandro Portes).

Robert Lima, born in 1935 in Havana, is a multitalented educator, poet, translator, literary critic, bibliographer, traveler, and biographer. In 1957, he earned his B.A. at Villanova University in English, Philosophy and History; in 1961 he received his M.A. from the same school in Theatre and Drama; and in 1968 was awarded a Ph.D. in Romance Languages and Literatures at New York University. At the same time he was studying, he was part of the New York City poetry scene, there he read weekly at the Judson Memorial Church, Café Cino, the "Tenth Street Coffeehouse", and other venues. He also performed occasionally at "La Mama" and other stages in the city, and co-edited the anthology, *Seventh Street: Poems of 'Les Derux Megots'*, the *Seventh Street Review*, and the second *Judson Review*.

After working in publishing, film and at The Voice of America, Lima's first professional academic appointment was at Hunter College of the City University of New York (CUNY). From 1965 until 2002, he taught at Pennsylvania State University, where he offered courses on Romanticism, the "Generation of 1898", 18$^{th}$ through 20$^{th}$ Century Drama, and Iberian Civilization and Culture, among others in the Comparative Literature Department, which he chaired from 1970 to 1975. Upon retirement after 40 years in the profession, he was named Professor Emeritus of Spanish and Comparative Literature, as well as Fellow Emeritus of Penn State's Institute for the Arts and Humanistic Studies.

Among his awards and honors are the following: he was a Cintas Fellow in Poetry; he was named a Senior Fullbright Fellow to Peru in 1976-77; in Cameroon, he was initiated as a Fon (tribal king) in the Menda-Nkwe nation in 1986. The Pennsylvania State University hosted "The Poetic World of Robert Lima. A Retrospective" in 2004; his poem "Astrals" won the first Phi Kappa Phi Poetry Competition in 2009; he was named Distinguished Alumnus by Villanova University. He was a member of Academia Norteamericana de la Lengua Española (the North America Academy of the Spanish Language) as well as of the Real Academia Española (the Royal Academy of Spain) and Academician of the Academia Norteamericana de la Lengua Española. He was inducted into the Enxebre Orden da Vieira in Madrid, Spain and, in the summer of 2003, was named Knight Commander of the Order of Queen Isabel of Spain by His Majesty King Juan Carlos 1.

He edited *Surrealism- A Celebration*, the papers of the international event he organized to commemorate the fiftieth anniversary of the movement, as a special volume of *The Journal of General Education* (1975). He co-revised *The Readers Encyclopedia of American Literature* (1962), and was contributing editor to *The McGraw-Hill Encyclopedia of World Drama* (1972).

Creatively, Robert Lima focused on drama and poetry. His play *Episode in Sicily* was premiered at a UNESCO Drama Festival and a second play, *The Lesson* was chosen by The Maryknoll Play Library for use by community theatres abroad. He translated Valle-Inclan's *Blood Pact*, which appeared in *Modern International Drama* and, with three other of his plays, in *Savage Acts, Four Plays* (1993). His translations of Bellido's *Bread and Rice*, or *Geometry in Yellow*, and Valle-Inclan's *Sacrilege* have been performed in the U.S. and Canada, respectively.

Lima wrote 27 books (criticism, poetry, biography, translation and bibliography) and has published widely in U.S. and foreign periodicals. His current projects are a family memoir; a new critical assestment of Lorca; theatrical works, another on Jorge Luis Borges' stories; a book on his world travel experiences; and a book of anecdotes on writers, painters, musicians, critics, and others whom he met over the course of many years. He is also preparing several poetry collections for publication. (Preceding data taken from secureapps.libraries.psu.edu).

Ruben G. Rumbaut is Professor of Sociology at the University of California, Irvine. He was born in Havana and received his PhD. from Brandies University in 1978. Dr. Rumbaut was a Fellow at the Center for Advanced Study in the Behavioral Sciences at Stanford in 2000-01, and a Visiting Scholar at the Russell Sage Foundation in New York City in 1997-98. He is the Founding Chair of the Section on International Migration of the American Sociological Association, and an elected member of the ASA's Council and of the Sociological Research Association. He is a member of the Committee on Population of the National Academy of Sciences, the Committee on International Migration of the Social Science Research Council, and the MacArthur Research Network on Transitions to Adulthood and Public Policy.

An internationally-known scholar of immigration and refugee movements, he directed throughout the 1980s the principal studies of the migration and incorporation of refugees from Vietnam, Laos, and Cambodia who were settled in the United States in the aftermath of the Indochina War- the *Indochinese Health and Adaptation Research Project* and the *Southeast Asian Refugee Youth Study*. He has traveled to Vietnam and Cambodia, and earlier to Sierra Leone, where he organized a field project on international health and economic development.

In the 1990s, he served as academic advisor for a prime-time 10-part PBS television series *Americas*, focusing on Latin American and Caribbean peoples. He also directed the first *National Survey of Immigration Scholars* in the United States, which generated new knowledge about the social origins and intellectual formation of the multidisciplinary field of international studies. He currently co-directs both the landmark Children of Immigrants Longitudinal Study (CILS), begun in 1991, and a new large-scale study of Immigration and Intergenerational Mobility in Metropolitan Los Angeles (IIMMLA).

He also edits (with Steven J. Gold), a research-oriented book series, "The New Americans: Recent Immigration and American Society", under their editorship more than 3 dozen titles have been published since 2002 on a wide range of immigration topics. Rumbaut is the author of more than one hundred scientific articles, monographs and chapters in scholarly volumes on the adaptation of immigrants and refugees in the United States. Professor Rumbaut has published a number of critically acclaimed books. He has published two companion books based on CILS (with Alejandro Portes): *Ethnicity: Children of Immigrants in America,* and *Legacies: The Story of the Immigrant Second Generation,* the latter of which won the American Sociological Association's top award in 2002 (the Sorokin Award for Distinguished Scholarship) as well as the 2002 Thomas and Znaniecki Award for best book in the immigration field.

He completed work with a panel of the National Academy of Sciences on two definite companion volumes on the Hispanic population of the United States in 2006, *Multiple Origins. Uncertain Destinies,* and *Hispanics and the Future of America.* (Preceding information taken from rumbautbio.pdf).

Miguel A. De La Torre is a Professor of Social Ethics and Latino/a Studies at IIff School of Theology in Denver, Colorado. He came to the United States from Cuba as an infant and was raised in New York City. He was baptized and confirmed in the Catholic Church although his parents were priest/priestess of the Santeria religion. He moved to Miami as a teenager and founded a real estate company called Championship Realty, Century 21.

He was very successful and the initial office grew to over 100 sales agents; during this time he obtained a Master's in Public Administration from American University in Washington, D.C. His success led him to be elected president of the Miami Board of Realtors. In his early twenties he became a "born-again" Christian, joining University Baptist Church in Coral Gables, Florida. De La Torre dissolved his real estate company in 1992 to attend Southern Baptist Theological Seminary in order to obtain a Master's in Divinity and enter the ministry. During his seminary training he served as pastor at a rural congregation in Glen Dean, Kentucky.

He later achieved a Doctorate from Temple University in Social Ethics. He focuses on ethics within contemporary U.S. thought, specifically how religion affects race, class, and gender oppression. His works (1) applies a social scientific approach to Latino/a religiosity within this country, (2) studies Liberation theologies in the Caribbean and Latin America (specifically in Cuba), and (3) engages in postmodern/postcolonial social theory.

De La Torre has authorized numerous articles and books, including several books that have won national awards, specifically *Reading the Bible from the Margins* (2002), *Santeria the Beliefs and Rituals of a Growing Religion in America* (2004), *Doing Christian Ethics from the Margins* (2004), and *Encyclopedia on Hispanic American Religious Culture, Volume 1 & 2* (2009).

He has served as a director to the Society of Christian Ethics and the American Academy of Religion. Additionally, he has been co-chair of the Ethics Section at the American Academy of Religion. He is the founder and editor of the *Journal of Race, Ethnicity, and Religion*. De La Torre has been an expert commentator concerning ethical issues (mainly Hispanic religiosity, LGBT civil rights), and immigration rights on several local, national, and international media outlets. He also writes monthly articles for Ethics Daily which creates controversies within Christian circles. During the January, 2011 gathering of the Society of Christian Ethics, he was elected Vice-President of the organization and President-elect for 2012.

Jorge J.E. Gracia is the Samuel P. Capen Chair, SUNY Distinguished Professor in the Department of Philosophy and Department of Comparative Literature in the State University of New York at Buffalo. Gracia was educated in Cuba, Canada and the United States and received his Ph.D. in Medieval Philosophy from the University of Toronto.

He has authored and edited over 40 books, his areas of specialization include Metaphysics/Ontology, Philosophical Historiography, Philosophy of Language/Hermeneutics, Ethnicity/Race Nationality Issues, Hispanic/Latino Issues, Medieval/Scholastic Philosophy and Hispanic/Latino/Latin-American Philosophy.

His contributions to the philosophical study of race and ethnicity have been groundbreaking. It is within this area that Gracia proposed his familial-historical view of ethnicity and his genetic common-bundle view of race. These views of race and ethnicity have helped to shape the field and addressed many issues that previous theories had left unanswered.

Gracia was the founding chair of the APA Committee for Hispanics in Philosophy, past president of the Society for Medieval and Renaissance Philosophy, past president of the Society for Iberian and Latin American Thought, past president of the American Catholic Philosophical Association, and past president of the Metaphysical Society of America.

Among his many awards are National Endowment for the Humanities Research Fellowship, 1981-82, John N. Findlay Prize in Metaphysics, awarded by the Metaphysical Society of America in 1992 for Individuality: An Essay on the Foundations of Metaphysics (1998), Aquinas Medal, awarded by the University of Dallas, on February 1, 2002, University of Buffalo Teaching and Learning Award, 2003 67th Aquinas Lecture at Marquette University, 2003 Director, National Endowment for the Humanities Summer Institute, Oct 1, 2004-Sept 31, 2005 Director, National Endowment for the Humanities Summer Seminar, Oct 1, 2005- Sept 31, 2006, "We the People Project".

Teófilo F. Ruiz is Distinguished Professor of History and Peter H. Reill Term Chair in European History at UCLA. Ruiz achieved a B.A. in The City College of the City of New York in 1969, a M.A. from New York University in 1970, and a PhD. from Princeton University in 1974. His field of specialization is Medieval, Early Modern Europe.

On February 12, 2012, it was announced that President Barack Obama would award Ruiz the National Humanities Medal. The award honors individuals or groups whose work has deepened the nation's understanding of the humanities, broadened the engagement of American citizens in the humanities, or helped preserve and expand access to important resources in the humanities.

A scholar who specializes in the social and cultural history of late medieval and early modern Spain, Ruiz was selected for his "inspired teaching and writing", according to the announcement issued by the White House. Ruiz has published, or has in press, 13 books and has written more than 60 articles in scholarly journals and hundreds of reviews and smaller articles. His book, "The Terror of History: On the Uncertainties of Life in Western Civilization", reflects on Western humanity's efforts to cope with and make meaning of the world and its disturbing history. The book was praised by Inside Higher Education for its "enormous erudition". He also co-edited in 2011 a volume that gathered 18th century Franciscan friar Junipero Serra's personal accounts of his voyages in California. The book was published in Spain.

Ruiz was born in Cuba in 1943 to descendants of immigrants from Spain's Old Castile region (today's province of Burgos), which has figured prominently in his scholarship. As a teenager, he was active in the Cuban Revolution, which overthrew the regime of Fulgencio Batista. But after a friend was killed in 1960, he broke ties with the revolution and was imprisoned. Following the failed Bay of Pigs invasion in 1961, he was released to make room for new political prisoners. Ruiz left for Miami that year, with "only three changes of clothing, $45, a box of Cuban cigars to sell and a Spanish translation of Jacob Burckhardt's , "A History of Greek Civilization".

By 1962, Ruiz and two cousins moved from Miami to New York City, where he worked at various jobs, including as a taxi driver. Despite many obstacles, he received his Doctorate from Princeton in 1974. Ruiz joined UCLA's faculty in 1998 after teaching at Brooklyn College, the City University of New York Graduate Center, the University of Michigan, and the Ecole des Hautes Etudes en Sciences Sociales in Paris.

Ruiz has received many accolades during his career. He has been the recipient of fellowships from the National Endowment for the Humanities, the Andrew W. Mellon Foundation, the Guggenheim Memorial Foundation, the Institute for Advanced Study, and the American Council of Learned Societies (ACLS). He was selected as one of four outstanding Teachers of the Year in the United States for 1994-95 by the Carnegie Foundation, and in 2008, he was honored as a UCLA Distinguished Teacher. (Preceding information taken from www.history.ucla.edu and newsroom.ucla.edu).

Jorge I. Domínguez was born in Cuba in 1945 and received his B.A. from Yale University in 1967 and earned his M.A. (1968) and Ph.D. (1972) from Harvard University. Dr. Dominguez is presently Vice Provost for International Affairs, Chairman, Harvard Academy for International and Area Studies, and Antonio Madero Professor for the Study of Mexico, Harvard University.

Among his numerous books are *Cuban Economic and Social Development: Policy Reforms and Challenges in the 21st Century* (co-ed. O.F. Perez, M. Espinal, and L. Barberia) 2012, *Debating U.S.-Cuban Relations: Shall We Play Ball,* (co-ed. R. Hernandez and L. Barberia) 2011, *Consolidating Mexico's Democracy: The 2006 Presidential Campaign in Comparative Perspective,* (co-ed. C. Lawson and A. Moreno) 2009.

Dominguez has written many other books and articles on domestic and international politics in Latin America and the Caribbean.

A past president of the Latin American Studies Association and a past board chairman of the Latin American Scholarship Program, he currently serves on the editorial boards of *Political Science Quarterly, Foreign Affairs Latinoamericana, Cuban Studies, Foro Internacional,* and *Journal of Cold War Studies.* He was series editor for the Peabody Award-winning Public Broadcasting System television-series *Crisis in Central America.* His current research focuses on the international relations and domestic politics of Latin American countries. (Preceding information taken from www.people.fas.harvard.edu).

Gregory Rabassa was born in 1922 in Yonkers, New York into a family headed by a Cuban immigrant. He is a literary translator from Spanish and Portuguese to English who has taught at Queens College. As of this writing (March 2013), he is still working at age 91. After serving in World War II as an OSS cryptographer and receiving a Bachelor's degree from Darmouth, Rabassa enrolled as a graduate student at Columbia University, where he earned a Doctorate. He taught at Columbia for over two decades before accepting a position at Queens College in New York. He has also taught at City College of New York and in the Ph.D. Program in Hispanic and Luso-Brazilian Literatures of the Graduate School and University Center of the CUNY Graduate Center.

Rabassa works primarily in Spanish and Portuguese; he has produced English-language versions of the works of several major Latin American novelists, including Julio

Cortazar, Jorge Amado and Gabriel Garcia Marquez. On the advice of Cortazar, Garcia Marquez waited three years for Rabassa's schedule to become open so that he could translate *One Hundred Years of Solitude*. He later commented Rabassa's translation to be superior to his own Spanish original.

He received the PEN Translation Prize in 1977 and the PEN/Ralph Manheim Medal for Translation in 1982. Rabassa was honored with the Gregory Kolovakos Award from PEN American Center for the expansion of Hispanic Literature to an English-language audience in 1991. For his version of Cortazar's novel, *Hopscotch*, Rabassa shared the inaugural United States National Book Award in category Translation. Rabassa retired from Queens College as Distinguished Professor Emeritus. In 2006, he was awarded the National Medal of Arts.

Rabassa typically translates without reading the book beforehand, working as he goes. He has written a memoir detailing his experiences as a translator, *If This Be Treason: Translation and Its Dyscontents, A Memoir*, a *Los Angeles Times* "Favorite Book of the Year" for 2005. Rabassa received the PEN/Martha Albrand Award for the Art of the Memoir for the book in 2006.

Yusnier Viera is President and Founder of Spicy Math and a Guinness World Record holder in calendar calculations. Known as the "Human Calculator", he has been teaching math for more than 10 years. Yusnier was born in Cuba and possesses a Bachelor's degree in Computer Science and a Master's in Mathematics.

Viera earned his nickname because of his amazing skills for calculating the day of the week for any date. His current World Record is for the greatest number of days of the week correctly identified from random dates in one minute. On December 4, 2010, he was able to identify 93 dates in one minute.

Yusnier speaks to educators and students about the importance of math in life. His mission is to help them understand that math can be fun and show them the best techniques in order to improve their math skills. In 2011 he was nominated International Ambassador for "World Math Day" due to his important contributions to mental calculations. (Preceding information taken from spicy-math.com).

George J. Borjas is the Robert W. Scrivner Professor of Economics and Social Policy at the Harvard Kennedy School. He is the recipient of the 2011 IZA Prize in Labor Economics. Professor Borjas is also a Research Associate at the National Bureau of Economic Research and a Research Fellow at IZA. He received his Ph.D. in Economics from Columbia University in 1975. Prior to moving to Harvard in 1995, he was a Professor of Economics at the University of California at San Diego. Borjas was born in Havana in 1950 and migrated to the United States in 1962.

Dr. Borjas is the author of several books, including *Wage Policy in the Federal Bureaucracy* (1980), *Friends or Strangers: The Impact of Immigrants on the U.S. Economy* (1990), *Heaven's Door: Immigration Policy and the American Economy* (1999), and the widely used textbook *Labor Economics 2012*, now in its sixth edition. He has published over 125 articles in books and scholarly journals. His work also appears regularly in major magazines and newspapers, including articles in *The Atlantic Monthly* and *Nation-*

*al Review,* as well as editorials in *The New York Times, The Wall Street Journal,* and *Le Monde.*

His professional honors include citations in *Who's Who in the World, Who's Who in America, Who's Who in Finance and Industry, Who's Who in Economics,* and research grants from the National Science Foundation, the Sloan Foundation, the Russell Sage Foundation, and the Smith-Richardson Foundation.

Professor Borjas' research on the economic impact of immigration is widely perceived as playing a central role in the debate over immigration policy in the United States and abroad. *Business Week* and *The Wall Street Journal,* in a front-page feature article, have called him "America's leading immigration economist". A cover story in *The New York Times Magazine* focused on his work, and called him "the pre-eminent scholar in his field". (Preceding information taken from www.hks.harvard.edu).

History professor Dr. Jaime Suchlicki has been selected as one of the top "100 Latinos in Miami". Others include former FIU President Mitch Maidique; President of Miami Dade College Eduardo Padron; singer Gloria Estefan; TV personality Oscar Haza; painter Romero Britto; baseball player Mike Lowell and television personality Don Francisco.

The selection was conducted by the Fundacion Fusionarte of Spain, a prominent Spanish group specializing in minorities in Europe, Latin America and the U.S. A book with the biographies of the nominees was published in October 2010 by the Foundation.

Dr. Suchlicki is Emilio Bacardi Moreau Distinguished Professor of History and Director of the Institute for Cuban and Cuban-American Studies at the University of Miami. His parents both emigrated to Cuba; his father from Poland in 1921 and his mother from Argentina in 1909. Suchlicki was a Law student at the University of Havana from 1959-60. He finished his undergraduate and graduate degrees at the University of Miami. He earned a Ph.D. from Texas Christian University and returned to teach at the University of Miami. He is the author of Mexico: From Montezuma to the Rise of the PAN (2008), Cuba: From Columbus to Castro and Beyond (2002), now in its 5th edition; Mexico: From Montezuma to the Fall of the PRI (2001); and Mexico: From Montezuma to the NAFTA and Beyond (2000). In 2008, his book, Breve Historia de Cuba, was selected as the year's outstanding Hispanic book in the category of history and politics. Dr. Suchlicki is a highly regarded consultant to the private and public sector on Cuba and Latin American affairs. (Preceding information taken from www.as.miami.edu).

Hilario Candela is the architect of the iconic Miami Marine Stadium. He designed it in 1962 in his twenties as a refugee while at the architectural firm Pancoast, Ferendino, Skeels, Grafton and Burnham. He became President of this firm which evolved into Spillis Candela-at one time the largest Hispanic owned architectural firm in the United States. The company was repeatedly included in the list of the largest 50 design firms in the United States by ENR.

Candela designed many buildings throughout the United States from New York to California, much of Latin America and the Caribbean as well as Spain and Saudi Arabia. Spillis Candela designed many structures in South Florida, including three campuses of Miami Dade College.

He is also a Co-Founder of Friends of Miami Marine Stadium and has been involved in the organization since its inception. The 6,566 seat stadium was considered a Modernist icon because of its cantilevered, fold-plate roof and construction of lightweight, poured-in-place concrete, popular in mid-century stadiums.

# Public Servants/Political-Military Figures

María Dolores Sánchez, better known as Lola Sanchez (1844-1895), was a Cuban-American Confederate spy during the Civil War. Lola was born in Armstrong, Florida, one of five siblings. Prior to 1850 the Sanchez family immigrated from Cuba and settled on the east bank of the St. Johns River in an area known as Federal Point opposite Palatka, Florida, a town situated about 63 miles south of Jacksonville.

So how did Lola end up as a Confederate spy? Apparently Sanchez became upset when her father was falsely accused of being a Confederate spy by members of the Union Army and imprisoned. Officers of the Union Army then occupied the Sanchez residence in Palatka. One night she overheard various officers planning a raid and decided to alert the Confederate forces. She informed Captain John Jackson Dickison, commander of the local Confederate forces, of the plan. The result of her action was that the Confederate forces surprised the Union troops in an ambush and captured the USS Columbine, a Union warship, on the day of the supposed raid in the "Battle of Horse Landing". This was one of the few instances in which a

Union warship was captured by land-based Confederate forces during the Civil War.

The story does not end just with Lola's involvement in this military action. Two of her sisters also became Confederate spies. While Lola was on her way to warn Captain Dickison, her sisters agreed to help by covering up her absence. Panchita entertained the troops while Eugenia prepared supper with the supposed assistance of Lola. Sanchez left the house that night and travelled, through the forest, alone on horseback. When she reached the ferry, the ferryman agreed to mind her horse while she crossed the river. After reaching the other side she came upon a Confederate sentry and told him what she had heard, but the sentry was unable to leave his post and lent her his horse. She then proceeded to the camp where she met with Dickison and told him what she knew. She then returned home, the entire ordeal took one and a half hours, and her absence went unnoticed by the Union soldiers.

That night captain Dickison and his men crossed the St, Johns River and set a trap. They waited for the arrival of the Union transport and gunboat. The Confederate military had placed artillery guns on the banks of the river and opened fire on the approaching Union gunboats. The confrontation which followed, officially known as the "Battle of Horse Landing", occurred south of St. Augustine. The USS Columbine was disabled and set on fire. Of the 148 men aboard the Columbine, only 66 survived and the rest were killed. The Confederates also captured a Union pontoon boat and renamed it "The Three Sisters" in honor of the Sanchez sisters.

Shortly thereafter Lola's sister Panchita decided to plead for their father's release from prison. She traveled to St. Augustine where she pleaded for her father's freedom. Panchita offered to take his place in exchange for his freedom. After listening to her plea, the prison authorities let her father go and they both were allowed to return home. The spy activities of the sisters, which continued during the duration of the war, were never discovered by the Union Army.

All three sisters married former Confederate officers. Lola was married to Emmanuel Lopez and had a daughter named Leonicia Lopez born in St. Augustine. Lola died in 1895 and was buried in Palatka. Lola's sister Panchita married Captain John R. Miot and moved to South Carolina; she had six children and was buried there in 1931. Eugenia married Albert Crespin Rogero, a former comrade of Emmanuel Lopez and lived in St. Augustine. She passed away on January 12, 1932 and is buried in Elkton, Florida.

In 1909, the State Convention of the United Daughters of the Confederacy was held in St. Augustine. The daughters of Lola and Panchita served as pages, in honor of their mothers' service to the Confederacy. The names of Lola Sanchez and her sisters appear in gold letters on a plaque with the names of 106 Confederate heroines that hangs in the United Daughters of the Confederacy Memorial Building in Richmond, Virginia.

An obituary in *The Miami Herald* dated March 17th, 2013, details the life of Sister Edith González, a Catholic nun who was much loved by those she served. She was described as a dear friend, a mother figure, and a confidante. She devoted her life to working with the perpetually underrepresented-children, AIDS patients, refugees, the impoverished in need of healthcare and the developmentally disabled. Sister Gonzalez lost a long battle with cancer at age 69.

Edith Carmen Gonzalez was born on September 20th, 1943, in Key West, Florida. Her parents were originally from Cuba and she attended Immaculata Academy and went on to receive a B.A. degree from the University of Miami and a Master's in Special Education from Barry University. While continuing her religious studies, Gonzalez spent five years in Italy working with the developmentally disabled. In 1987, she became a member of the Congregation of the Sisters of St. Joseph of St. Augustine. She later taught at St. Mary's Cathedral School in Miami.

She was instrumental in developing the AIDS program at Mercy Hospital in Miami during the early 1990s, which became one of the largest and most successful private AIDS programs in the country. She also brought the Legacy Institute to Mercy Hospital, a program that trains spiritual healthcare professionals to care for the underrepresented in a faithful environment. The Mercy program will be named after her. Gonzalez also worked with addiction recovery programs, impoverished families in Guatemala, Camillus House and San Juan Bosco Medical Clinic for the underprivileged.

Sister Gonzalez was known for her infinite compassion and objectivity. She often counseled families through the heart-wrenching decision of whether to keep a patient on life support. Among those patients was Pedro Zamora, one of the first openly gay men with AIDS who appeared in popular media, as part of the cast of *The Real World: San*

*Francisco* in 1994. Zamora's sister, Mily Zamora, said she and her family were struggling to come to terms with the terminal nature of AIDS. Gonzalez helped her understand that everyone has to die. It takes a special person to bring someone to that conclusion peacefully, Zamora said.

Florida State Senator Rene Garcia became friends with Gonzalez while he was in the Legislature, working to get funding for San Juan Bosco Medical Clinic. Gonzalez kept an eye on Garcia in the Senate, making sure he was doing the most good for his underrepresented constituents. *The Herald* piece notes that Garcia said she even called him in Tallahassee a few times to ask why he'd voted a certain way. She joked with the other nuns that she had her own senator. Garcia flew to Miami to see Gonzalez about three weeks before she died, when he heard her health was failing. He said her eyes welled with tears as they spoke, and she reminded him to remember his purpose in politics- to do the most good.

Carlos Pascual was born in Havana in 1959; he is the State Department's Special Envoy and Coordinator for International Energy Affairs. Secretary Clinton appointed Ambassador Pascual to this position, effective May 18, 2011. In this capacity, he advises the Secretary on energy issues, ensuring that energy security is advanced at all levels of U.S. foreign policy. Prior to his appointment, Pascual served as the United States Ambassador to Mexico (2009-2011) and was Vice President and Director of the Foreign Policy Studies Program at the Brookings Institute (2003-2009).

During his extensive career in public service Ambassador Pascual has held positions in the Department of State, the National Security Council (NSC) and the United States Agency for International Development (USAID). He served as Coordinator for Reconstruction and Stabilization at the U.S. Department of State, where he led and organized U.S. government planning to help stabilize and reconstruct societies in transition from conflict or civil strife.

Ambassador Pascual served as Coordinator for U.S. Assistance to Europe and Eurasia (2003), where he oversaw regional and country assistance strategies to promote market-oriented and democratic states. He also served as U.S. Ambassador to Ukraine (2000-2003), Special Assistant to the President and NSC Senior Director for Russia, Ukraine and Eurasia (1998-2000), and Director for the same region (1995-1998). Before that, Pascual worked for USAID in Sudan, South Africa and Mozambique and as Deputy Assistant Administrator for Europe and Eurasia (1983-1995).

He received his M.P.P. from the Kennedy School of Government at Harvard University in 1982 and his B.A. from Stanford University in 1980. He has served on the boards of directors for the National Endowment for Democracy, Freedom House, and the Internews Network. He has also served on the Advisory Group for the United Nations Peacebuilding Fund. (Preceding information taken from www.state.gov.).

Caridad Asencio was the co-founder of the Caridad Center, Boyton Beach, Florida's largest free clinic. She was born in Cuba and fled to New York City soon after the communist regime took power. Asencio's first name means "charity" in Spanish, but her legacy translates to a level of medical and social services to the Palm Beach County working poor that was unprecedented.

A social worker and educator, Asencio met fellow schoolteacher and clinic co-founder Constance Berry in 1979. Many of the schoolchildren the women taught were from farm worker families in dire need of medical and dental care, food, clothing and homework help. The two women founded the Migrant Association of South Florida in 1989 to help the children and provide housing to agricultural workers and their families.

Three years later, they started a free clinic in a modest doublewide trailer at U.S. 441 in Boyton Beach, Fla., with the help of volunteer doctors and dentists. The pair soon began raising funds from local donors to purchase land and built a 7,500 square-foot building in Boyton Beach, a few miles east of the original location.

Asencio provided outreach any way she could to the people who needed it most and she ultimately put the "other side" of Palm Beach County on the map: the undocumented workers, the working poor, the sick, the families who fell between the cracks of America's social system. She started an organization that not only gave hope to the poor, but also began to turn their lives around. In the past few decades that organization redefined healthcare in Palm Beach County, and has become a model for humanitarian outreach.

In 2010, more than 24, 500 patient visits were made from 6,500 unduplicated patients who utilized Caridad's free medical, dental and vision clinics through the expertise and dedication of more than 400 volunteers, providing health and social services to the community.

Her work was widely recognized. In 2010, she was inducted in the 2010/2011 Florida Women's Hall of Fame by the Florida Commission on the Status of Women. She was also a Junior League Woman Volunteer of the Year. National awards included the Presidential Volunteer Service Award, Common Cause Annual Public Service Award and the National Jefferson Award, among others. Caridad Asencio passed away October 29, 2011, at age 79. ( Preceding information taken from caridad.org).

Adolph (Adolfo) Fernández Cavada and his brother Frederick (Federico) Fernández Cavada were born in Cienfuegos, Cuba, sons of a Cuban father and Emily Howard, a native of Philadelphia. When their father died, the boys and their mother moved to Pennsylvania. They were educated in private schools and graduated from Central High School in Philadelphia.

At the outbreak of the American Civil War, Adolph and Frederick enlisted in the Union forces, serving as Captains of various companies in the Philadelphia 23$^{rd}$ PA Infantry Regiment. Adolph served with distinction in the Army of the Potomac from Fredericksburg to Gettysburg and was a "special aide-de-camp" to General Andrew Humphries. Frederick transferred to the 114$^{th}$ PA Infantry Regiment, rising to the rank of Lieutenant Colonel. Frederick gained notoriety as well from his writings, sketches, and paintings related to his incarceration as a prisoner of war in the infamous Libby Prison in Richmond, Virginia. In a poem by Frederick in 1862, he writes, "I have pulled through many a march, I have been in many a battle, I have seen the bomb shell burst, I have heard the grapeshot rattle! With the bravest, in the strife, I have nobly risked my life".

One of the most vivid and articulate accounts of the Battle of Gettysburg comes from the pen of Adolph, who kept a diary during the war. His eyewitness account of the famous conflict provides a highly descriptive and informative rendition of the heroism and horror, sights and sounds of battle. During one day of the July battle, he recorded how "the air was soon full of flying shot shell and canister-and a groan here and there attested their affect...the roar of musketry and the bursting shells was deafening..."

Though raised in Philadelphia, both brothers continued to maintain a strong connection to their native isle of Cuba. After the Civil War, the Federal government appointed the brothers to consular positions-Frederick in Trinidad and Adolph in Cienfuegos. During the War of Cuban Independence, which broke out in 1868, the two brothers resigned from their commissions and became actively involved in the Cuban Army of Liberation from Spain. Both became officers in the uprising, yet both brothers would lose their lives in the fight for Cuban independence.

Frederick, called the "Fire King"by the Spanish authorities during the War of Cuban Independence, was captured, court-martialed, and sentenced with the rumor he was to be hanged. Many of his former friends and military compatriots with whom he'd served in the Union Army-including Generals George Gordon Meade, Daniel Sickles and Ulysses S. Grant, attempted to obtain his release without success.

In July 1871, Frederick Fernandez Cavada was taken to Puerto Principe and executed. During the hour of his death, it was reported that he calmly conversed with some friends, smoked a cigar, and walked erect and proud to the place of execution where he flung his hat to the ground "and in a loud tone of voice cried, "*Adios Cuba, para siempre*" (Goodbye Cuba, forever). After this, a volley was fired and he was killed. (Preceding information taken from pacivilwar150.com).

Havana native Alex Castellanos has nearly four decades of political and private sector consulting experience in the United States and around the globe. Castellanos has developed communication strategies and campaigns for some of the world's largest companies and helped elect U.S. Senators, Governors and Presidents. He co-founded Purple Strategies, a bipartisan public affairs firm, appears regularly on Meet the Press and currently serves as a member of CNN's "Best Political Team on Television".

In 2007, GQ Magazine named him one of the 50 Most Influential People in D.C. He has been a Fellow at the Institute of Politics at the Kennedy School of Government at Harvard University. He has also been credited with his discovery of the political "soccer-mom" and called "father of the attack ad".

Castellanos is fluent in Spanish and English; his parents, refugees who fled Castro's Cuba in 1961, came to this country with one suitcase, two children and eleven dollars.

An article in *Daily Business Review* dated March 18th, 2013, profiles a Miami judge. Jorge E. Cueto is a Miami-Dade Circuit Judge who took a rather interesting and long road before wearing the black robes. He was born in Cuba and his family came to Miami when he was 4 years old. He attended Boston University and the University of Miami where he studied chemistry and biochemistry. He was considering getting a Doctorate in biochemistry when he realized funding for the sciences was drying up.

According to the publication he dove into mortgage banking, which "was the best job I ever had because I got paid to eat and drink and socialize. And if you know me, I like to do all three." But as interest rates climbed from 6 percent to 16 plus percent, business dried up rather quickly. He then saw a television ad soliciting applicants for Miami-Dade Police Department. He applied, was accepted and spent 16 years, learning about people, police and himself. He started as a patrol officer, spent several years in internal affairs and finally served as general investigations commander for the Cutler Ridge district.

Restless about his career options, he decided to study law. He got his J.D. at the University of Miami while working as a police sergeant. Three years later, the department assigned him to work with the Miami-Dade County Commission as staff counsel to the public safety committee. In 1998, he left to become vice president and in-house counsel for an engineering company outside of Chicago. His duties included legal affairs, contract negotiating, and accounting. He also oversaw production, corporate communications, inventory control and management, information technologies, human resources, purchasing and more. He also handled two mergers and acquisitions.

Six years later, his in-laws' failing health brought him and his wife back to Miami. He joined the Miami-Dade State Attorney's office and quickly moved into the high-profile public corruption unit. In 2008, he ran for judge and won. Now he arrives at work between 6:20 and 6:30 AM "and has been known to call special set hearings at 6 AM." He is quoted as stating that he reads everything submitted to him, "footnotes and all. "I think people know where I'm coming from", he said. 'They know that I'm ready and when you come in here you'd better be ready because I don't suffer fools lightly or gladly".

Joseph E. Miro, born in Matanzas, Cuba in 1946, is a Republican member of the Delaware House of Representatives, representing the 22nd District since 1998. He served on the New Castle County Council from 1992-1998. Miro is currently the President of Miro Diversified Services, and was a teacher in the Christina School District from 1970-2001. He is a member of the Government Hispanic Council Board, Foxfire Civic Association, Knights of Columbus, and Holy Angels Church. He is the President of the National Hispanic Caucus of State Legislatures.

Cecilia Maria Altonaga is a Florida United States District Court Judge. She is the first Cuban-American woman to be appointed as a federal judge in the United States. She was born in Baltimore, Maryland and received her B.A. from Florida International University in 1983; she then graduated from Yale Law School in 1986.

She worked as an attorney in the Miami Dade County Attorney's Office from 1986-1987, and then served as a law clerk to Edward B. Davis of the United States District Court for the Southern District of Florida from 1987-88 before returning to the County Attorney's Office until 1996. In 1996, Governor Lawton Chiles appointed her as a County Court Judge on Florida's Eleventh Judicial Circuit

Court. In 1999, she was elevated to Circuit Court Judge in that district by Governor Jeb Bush.

Altonaga was nominated for a seat on U.S. District Court for the Southern District of Florida by George W. Bush on January 15, 2003, to a seat vacated by Shelby Highsmith. She was confirmed by the U.S. Senate on May 6, 2003 and received her commission the following day. During her time on the federal bench, Altonaga has been noted for her strong support of the recently created Florida International University College of Law, having served as the keynote speaker in the 2004 Convocation, judged several moot court competitions, and employed FIU law students as summer interns.

Havana-born George Gascón is the District Attorney for the City and County of San Francisco. He has earned a national reputation as a criminal justice visionary and as a leader who uses evidence based practices to make communities safer by lowering crime. He is the first Latino to hold the office in San Francisco and is the nation's first police chief to become District Attorney.

District Attorney Gascon was elected on an agenda to transform the criminal justice system and make San Francisco the safest large city in America. His approach to public safety and reform is based on the need to hold people accountable without breaking the wallets of California taxpayers. He created the nation's first Alternative Sentencing Program to support prosecutors in assessing risk to determine the most appropriate course of action in each case. The goal is to protect victims and the community by addressing offenders' risk factors to break the cycle of crime and recidivism.

A former high school dropout, Gascon understands the importance of keeping kids in school to reduce violence and prevent crime. In partnership with the San Francisco Unified School District, the District Attorney's Office has launched innovative programs to reduce truancy, increase mentoring opportunities for youth, and reduce bullying.

George Gascon has thirty years of experience in law enforcement promoted through the ranks to become Assistant Chief at the Los Angeles Police Department, Chief of Police in Mesa, Arizona and Chief of Police in San Francisco. He has also worked public safety initiatives in Latin America and the Middle East. He is a Board member of the Council of State Government's Justice Center, is a graduate of the FBI's National Executive Institute, and is a member of the Harvard/Kennedy School of Government's Executive Session on Policing and Public Safety. He has a B.A. in History from California State University, Long Beach, and a Juris Doctor degree from Western State University, College of Law. (Preceding information taken from www.sfdistrictattorney.org).

Jorge Mas Canosa was born in Santiago de Cuba in 1939. There he attended elementary and high school, moving then to the United States for a short period where he attended the Presbyterian Junior College of North Carolina before returning to Cuba to pursue a degree in law at the University of Oriente. Following months of intense struggle as a student leader in Cuba, first against the Batista dictatorship and then against Castro's communism, he was arrested and persecuted for his democratic ideals until he was given no other choice but to seek exile. In Miami, he joined the ranks of Brigade 2506 and following the failed Bay of Pigs invasion, graduated as a Second Army Lieutenant at Fort Benning, Georgia.

In Miami, he married Irma Santos, his high school sweetheart. Through much work and sacrifice, he became a successful businessman. He founded his first company, Church and Tower in Perrine, Florida. That company went on to become MasTec, a multinational corporation, still headquartered in Miami, once named the largest U.S.-Hispanic owned business in the country and the first Hispanic owned corporation to be featured on the New York Stock Exchange (NYSE). The company today employs over 8,000 people around the globe.

Among the numerous honors and awards he was bestowed, Jorge Mas Canosa received an honorary doctorate from Mercy College of New York for "exceptional work on behalf of democracy and human rights". The U.S. Department of Education granted him the "Lincoln-Marti" award for "excellence in civic contributions to the United States of America." In 1991, the Puerto Rican Senate, paid homage to him for his "valiant struggle in favor of returning democracy to his homeland of Cuba." Another great honor was his naming to the Presidential Advisory Board for Broadcasting which was charged with supervising Radio and Television Marti. He served in this capacity until his death in 1997. Mas Canosa was also named as President of the Governmental Commission for a Free Cuba in the state of Florida.

He not only dedicated himself to the cause of freedom for his native Cuba, but contributed generously to, and was a very active member of, his community in South Florida. He served on various local Boards including the

Miami Chamber of Commerce, YMCA of Dade-County, the "Plus Ten" Club of the Miami-Dade United Way, and the Hispanic Business Owners Association.

In 1981, he established the Cuban American National Foundation, a non-profit organization, that not only worked towards influencing U.S. policy towards Cuba and promoting democracy and human rights, but that has made numerous contributions to the local community. In 1992, for example, when Hurricane Andrew devastated South Florida, Jorge Mas Canosa and the CANF coordinated an intense relief effort, targeting in particular those communities in the southern part of Miami Dade County. That effort lasted well over six months after the hurricane hit and was responsible for distributing aid to thousands of affected families.

In 1997, Jorge Mas Canosa purchased the Freedom Tower, the historic downtown building that had once served as a processing center for thousands of Cuban refugees (I recall going there shortly after arriving in Miami.) After years of abandonment, the building had become structurally unsafe and was rotting away. Realizing the importance the building held for the community, Jorge Mas Canosa not only saved the building by purchasing it, but spent tremendous resources in restoring the tower to its former beauty. (Preceding information from www. jorgemascanosa.org.)

Rosario Kennedy (born Rosario Arguelles y Freyre de Andrade), was the first Cuban American woman on the City of Miami Commission, former Vice Mayor of the City of Miami and candidate for Florida's 18th Congressional district in 1989 to replace Claude Pepper that was eventually won by Ileana Ros-Lehtinen. Kennedy was the daughter of a former senator of Cuba and her grand uncle was Mario Garcia Menocal, a past President of the island nation.

In 1960, at age 14 Rosario arrived in the United States; she graduated with a scholarship from the Convent of the Sacred Heart in Greenwich, Connecticut. At 17 she married Gustavo Godoy Andrews, who would become news director at WLTV Channel 23 in Miami. By the time she was 25 Kennedy was divorced and became a real estate agent ultimately being named in 1979, "Business Woman of the Year" by the international business magazine *Mundo Latino*.

In 1978 she married former City of Miami Mayor David T. Kennedy. In 1988 she ran for the City of Miami Commission against the incumbent Demetrio Perez. She won the election and was later elected by her peers on the Commission as Vice Mayor. Today she owns Rosario Kennedy & Associates, Corp., a firm specializing in lobbying and governmental consultation to corporate clients, individuals, and professional associations before local, state, and federal governmental agencies.

Erneido Oliva is a retired Major General of the U.S. Army who was the deputy commander of Brigade 2506 land forces in the abortive Bay of Pigs Invasion of Cuba in April 1961. In 1954 Oliva was commissioned as a second lieutenant in the Cuban army after graduating from the Cuban Military Academy. From 1958 to 1959 he graduated with honors and was an instructor at the U.S. Army Caribbean School in the Canal Zone, Panama.

During the Bay of Pigs conflict, Oliva was captured by Cuban militia on April 23, 1961, and was released from prison and flown to Miami on December 24, 1962 after the U.S. Government paid a ransom of $500,000 for each of the three leaders of the Brigade.

Since his arrival in the United States, Oliva developed a close relationship with U.S. Attorney General Robert F. Kennedy. Bobby Kennedy involved him in the Cuban Project (*Operation Mongoose*), a White House-organized counterrevolutionary unit led by Manuel Artime based in Costa Rica and Nicaragua that staged commando raids on Cuban shore installations. In March 1963 Oliva was commissioned in the U.S. Army as a second lieutenant and was appointed by President Kennedy to represent Cuban-American personnel serving throughout the U.S. armed forces. At the White House on February 1964, in the presence of the then Attorney General Robert Kennedy, President Johnson informed Oliva of his decision to end all Cuban anti-Castro projects sponsored by the government including the one led by Oliva in U.S. Army. Oliva underwent infantry training at Fort Benning, Georgia, and artillery training at Fort Sill, Oklahoma. He participated in the U.S. intervention in the Dominican Republic where he served over a year. In 1969, he requested to be transferred to the U.S. Army Reserve.

In 1970, he joined the District of Columbia National Guard as a major. In August 1984, Oliva was promoted to Brigadier General of the line in the U.S. Army Reserve and commanded a Military Police Brigade. He earned a Master's degree in International Affairs from the American University in Washington, D.C., and attended the Program for Senior Executives in National and International Security at Harvard University.

In July 1987, U.S. President Ronald Reagan appointed him to the position of Deputy Commanding General of the D.C. Army National Guard. In December 1992, he was promoted to Major General in the District of Columbia Army National Guard. He retired on January 1, 1993 and has remained active in the anti-Castro effort, though largely steering clear of exile politics. In January 2008, he was honored with the Heritage Award, a nationally recognized award of Heroes and Heritage which was presented to him by the Vice-Chairman of the Joint Chiefs of Staff. He was later appointed by President George W. Bush to serve as a member of the Board of Governors of the United States Organizations, Incorporated (USO) for a three year term.

Katherine Fernández-Rundle was appointed State Attorney for Miami-Dade County in 1993. She has subsequently been re-elected five times to serve as State Attorney. She has a long history of involvement in her community and her state that date back to her days at Miami Palmetto High School and her undergraduate career at the University of Miami. She went on to obtain her law degree from the prestigious Cambridge University in England. State Attorney Fernandez-Rundle prides herself in being a career crime fighter and prides herself with the fact that her office has attained the highest percentage of convictions in cases involving public corruption in the State of Florida. She is recognized as a pioneer in the creation of numerous programs dealing with issues that affect the community daily such as teen truancy, domestic violence, child support, and victim's rights.

She served as the first and only Hispanic female on the State Constitutional Revision Council. Her passion and interest in public service is in large part due to the inspiration of her father, Dr. Carlos Benito Fernandez, one of Miami's first Hispanic judges and a founder of the Cuban American Bar Association, the largest Hispanic legal organization of which Ms. Fernandez-Rundle was elected president in 1991.

As the legal arm of the 37 different police departments in the county, the office's mission is to see that the guilty are convicted while the rights of the innocent are protected. The office is the fourth largest district attorney's office in the nation with over 1,300 employees, 300 of them prosecutors also known as Assistant State Attorneys. In addition to seeing that justice is carried out, her office is the only prosecutor's office in the state that protects the rights of children with the creation and enforcement of a strict child support program that annually processes over 90,000 cases.

Other innovative programs to help prevent crime and provide rehabilitative opportunities such as Drug Court, the Juvenile Gun Offenders Program, and the Second Chance Sealing and Expungement programs have all been established under the direction of State Attorney Katherine Fernandez-Rundle.

She is a founding member and Vice-President of Women of Tomorrow, a mentoring program that looks to inspire and motivate young at-risk high school women. Ms. Fernandez-Rundle is also very active in important organizations such as the Childrern's Services Council, 5000 Role Models of Excellence, Amigos for Kids, Mothers Against Drunk Driving (MADD), Habitat for Humanity, and numerous others. (Preceding information taken from cabaonline.com.)

Alicia C. Marill and Adriano García are two exceptional people whose passion is helping the poor and disadvantaged. The community of Amor en Accion was founded as a result of the missionary experiences of two of its members, Adriano and Alicia. They met in Miami in 1965 upon each returning from separate experiences of missions in the Dominican Republic. They felt a special call to dedicate their lives to missionary work through servicing the poor. They began to engage others to work with them; they founded Amor en Accion (Faith in Action) community, with the principle that *"faith without action is dead"* (James, 2:14). The group initially focused its efforts on the Dominican Republic and Mexico, and later in Haiti.

From the community's earliest stages, members dedicated themselves to promoting the Catholic faith in the missionary dimension of the Church, with the encouragement of then Archbishop Edward A. McCarthy. In 1976, the group was officially established as a lay missionary community, with his blessing and sponsorship. He enthusiastically supported Amor en Accion's vision of living out the universality of the Catholic faith, which led to the establishment of the Sister Diocese relationship with the Diocese of Port-de-Paix, in 1980.

An additional Sister community of Amor en Accion began in 1997 in the Diocese of Saginaw, Michigan, by Carmen Mora, a member who moved there and works in that diocese. Amor en Accion has touched thousands of lives in other countries and here at home. Today the missionary arm of the archdiocese of Miami with its Sister Diocese relationship with the Diocese of Port-de-Paix, also works with pastoral agents in Gros Morne, Haiti and in 5 areas of the Dominican Republic. Today Alicia Marill is Director and President of Amor en Accion, Inc., and Adriano Garcia serves as Director and Vice President. (Preceding information taken from amorenaccion,com).

Alejandro Mayorkas is the Director of United States Citizenship and Immigration Services (USCIS). Nominated by President Obama in April 2009, he was unanimously confirmed by the United States Senate in August 2009. As Director of USCIS, Mayorkas leads the agency within the U.S. Department of Homeland Security charged with operating the largest immigration system in the world. He is responsible for enhancing USCIS efforts to provide accurate and useful information to customers, grant immigration and citizenship benefits, promote an awareness and understanding of citizenship, and ensure the integrity of the immigration system. Director Mayorkas is responsible for an 18,000 member workforce throughout more than 200 offices worldwide and oversees a $3 billion annual budget.

Prior to his appointment as the Director of USCIS, Mayorkas was a partner in the law firm of O'Melveney & Myers LLP. He advised boards of directors and executives, led internal investigations, and litigated cases across a wide array of industries. He served as a member of O'Melveney & Myers' worldwide governing Policy Committee and as Chair of the firm's Values Awards Committee and the Warren Christopher Scholarship Committee. In 2008, *The National Law Journal* recognized Mayorkas as one of the "50 Most Influential Minority Lawyers in America".

In 1998, Senator Dianne Feinstein recommended Mayorkas to be the United States Attorney for the Central District of California. Nominated by President Clinton and confirmed by the U.S. Senate, he became the youngest U.S. Attorney to serve the nation at that time. Mayorkas led an office of 240 Assistant U.S. Attorneys and oversaw the prosecution of cases of national and international significance. He served as the Vice-Chair of the Attorney General's Advisory Subcommittee on Civil Rights and as a member of the Subcommittee on Ethics in Government.

From 1989 to 1998, Mayorkas served as Assistant U.S. Attorney for the Central District of California. Between 1996 and 1998, he additionally served as Chief of the Office's General Crime Section overseeing the training and trial work of new Assistant U.S. Attorneys in the Criminal Division. Throughout his twelve years as a federal prosecutor, he received numerous awards and commendations from federal and local law enforcement officials and agencies. He is a graduate of the University of California at Berkeley, and holds a J.D. from Loyola Law School. Mayorkas was born in Havana and came to the United States when he was one. Both of his parents were Jewish; his mother having fled from Romania to Cuba during World War II. ( Preceding information taken from uscis.gov ).

Carlos A. Giménez was reelected as Miami-Dade County's Mayor on August 14th, 2012. As the County's top elected official and chief administrator, Mayor Gimenez is responsible for the leadership and management of an organization with over 25,000 employees and an annual budget of nearly $6 billion.

Prior to this election, Mayor Gimenez served on the Miami-Dade Board of County Commissioners for seven years. He was first elected on November 2, 2004 and subsequently reelected for a second term without opposition in August 2008. As Commissioner for District 7, he represented numerous municipalities, including the City of Miami, the Village of Key Biscayne, the City of Coral Gables, the City of South Miami, the Village of Pinecrest, as well as areas of unincorporated Miami-Dade County.

From May 2000 to January 2003, Mayor Gimenez was Manager of the City of Miami and was credited with helping to restore stability and integrity to that organization. As Miami's Chief Administrator Officer, he was responsible for an annual budget of $500 million, a 4,000 employee workforce and provision of services to almost 400,000 residents. During his tenure as the City of Miami's top administrator, the City's bond rating went from "junk" to investment grade and the tax rate dropped to its lowest level in 50 years. At the same time, Miami was able to establish more than $140 million in reserves.

Prior to his appointment to City Manager, Gimenez spent 25 years with Miami's Fire-Rescue Department. The last nine of these years he served as the Chief of Fire-Rescue, during which time he was credited with modernizing the City's Fire Department and overseeing the largest reorganization in the department's history.

Mayor Gimemez earned his Bachelor's degree in Public Administration from Barry University in Miami. In 1993, he completed the Program for Senior Executives in State and Local Government at Harvard University's John F. Kennedy School of Government. Gimenez was born in Havana in 1954 and immigrated to the United States with his family in 1960. (Preceding information taken from miamidade.gov).

Lara Larramendi Blakely was born in Santiago de Cuba and came to the United States as a child in 1961. She has lived in California since 1963, owning a home in Monrovia since 1975. She earned her Bachelor's degree in Sociology from Cal State University at Los Angeles and earned her Master's from UCLA. She is the former Mayor of Monrovia, California; she was elected to the Monrovia City Council in 1988 and was reelected in 1990, 1994, and 1999.

She also served as a California State Assembly Speaker appointee to the Cost Control Performance Advisory Committee, a member of the Housing, Community, and Economic Development Policy Committee, which she later chaired from 1991-1994. Blakely was a member of the Environmental Quality Policy Committee, and served as a representative to a number of committees including the NLC CED Policy and Steering Committee, the Joint Committee on Youth Policy, the California Affordable Housing Partnership Project, and the Los Angeles County Metropolitan Transit Authority's Special Task Force for Countywide Bicycle Policy. She was also elected to the National League of Cities Board of Directors to a 2 year term in December 1994, was a past President of Women in Municipal Government, and a member of Hispanic Elected Local Officials.

Armando Valladares is an internationally known Cuban ex-political prisoner. In 1960, while working in the Office of the Ministry of Communications for the revolutionary government of Fidel Castro, he was arrested for openly expressing his disapproval of communism. Without any evidence or witnesses to accuse him, in less than a week he was sentenced to 30 years in prison; his only crime was having a different point of view and moral convictions. Refusing to succumb to the indoctrination of the prison's political rehabilitation program, he was subjected to torture, kept in isolation and in solitary confinement cells for long periods of time, even years.

Written on cigarette papers, he was able to clandestinely smuggle out his collection of poems so they could be published outside of Cuba and his work be known by intellectuals worldwide. The PEN Club of France honored him with the Freedom Prize, awarded to writers in prison. In several European countries, Valladares Committees were established to work on achieving his freedom. Amnesty International adopted him as a prisoner of conscience. The worldwide campaign spearheaded by his wife Martha resulted in French President Francois Mitterrand's personal petition to Fidel Castro, which resulted in his release after 22 years in prison on October of 1982. To put this in perspective, Valladares served more time in jail than what many murderers spend in the United States.

After his release, he wrote the international best seller, "Against All Hope", his memoirs based on his time in prison, which has been translated into 18 languages. After reading the book, President Ronald Reagan named him U.S. Ambassador to the U.N. Human Rights Commission where he demonstrated that in Cuba, as in all dictatorships, their exists torture and human rights violations. President Reagan also honored him with the Presidential "Citizen Medal", the second highest award given to a civilian in the United States. He was also bestowed The Superior Award by the U.S. Department of State. He has also been honored with the Italian Prize for International Journalism, the ISCHIA, and the Order of Jose Cecilio del Valle, the highest distinction granted to a foreigner by the president of Honduras. (Preceding information taken from armandovalladares.com).

## About the author

Fernando "Fernan" Hernandez was born in Banes, Cuba, on October 23, 1952. He and his older brother Luis left the island in 1962 when they were 9 and 11 years old, respectively via Operation Pedro Pan. After staying with a cousin in Miami for about 9 months, they went to live with a maternal aunt and her family in New York City until they were reunited with their parents. The separation from their mother and father lasted nearly four years.

The author is a graduate of Power Memorial Academy in Manhattan and St. Thomas University in Miami, Florida where he earned undergraduate and graduate degrees in Communication Arts and Management. He spent many years as a successful pharmaceutical salesman before he decided to pursue education. Fernando (Fernán) is Business Lead Instructor at Everest Institute, a nationally accredited career college. He has also taught at Carlos Albizu University's Business Department in Miami. He and his wife Josie have two adult children and make their home in Miami. When not teaching or writing, Fernán and Josie can be found horseback riding, canoeing, skiing or traveling. He is the author of Spanish-language books *Potaje* (www.alexlib.com/potaje, *Lo que aprendi de mi perro* (www.alexlib.com/miperro) and *The Cubans Our Legacy in the United States* (www.amazon.com). His short story, *Knutts' Cases*, about fictional psychiatrist Dr. R.U. Knutts, can be found in www.thewritedeal.org, His work also appears in the anthology *Un Horizonte Literario: Poesias, Cuentos y Algo Mas.*

The author welcomes readers' comments and opinions. He can be contacted in either English or Spanish at fernpa@hotmail.com.

# Index

## A

Abella, Alex 39
Aguabella, Francisco 88
Aguirre, Jessica 90
Alfonso, Ozzie 74
Almirola, Aric 111
Alonso, Alfredo 41
Alonso, Osvaldo 102
Altonaga, Cecilia María 246
Álvarez, Ana Cristina 50
Álvarez, Eddy 107
Álvarez, Isabel 118
Amorós, Sandy 100

Angones, Francisco 174
Anrrich, Graciela 171
Aponte, Midy 53
Arenas, Gilbert 110
Argiz, Antonio 'Tony" 179
Arner, Lucy 24
Asencio, Caridad 240
Asencio, Juan A. 193
Avellanet, Francisco 174
Azel, José 51, 173
Azpiazu, Don 19

## B

Balmaseda, Liz 40
Barrueco, Manuel 89
Batista, Alexis 125

Bechily, María 181
Blanco, Richard 13
Borjas, George J. 230

## C

Calvet, Cesar E. 175
Campo, Pupi 20
Canals Barrera, María 38
Candela, Hilario 232
Canete, ángel 141
Cano, Raúl 159
Canosa, Jorge Mas 248
Canto, Silvio 91

Carbonell, Manuel 25
Cárdenas, Leo 98
Carreño, José Manuel 59
Casarreal, Kenia 170
Castellanos, Agustín 196
Castellanos, Alex 244
Chapman, Aroldis 112
Child, Desmond 70

Chovel, Elly 138
Cisneros, Octavio 164
Codina, Armando 143
Conte, Luis 61
Cortada, Xavier 60
Coto, Manny 85
Cruz, Emilio 69

Cruz, Valerie 42
Cuellar, Mike 97
Cueto, Jorge E. 244
Curbelo, José 56
Curbelo, Silvia 84
Cutie, Alberto 13

**D**

Darby, Marta María 36
De Acosta Lydig, Rita 30
De Cárdenas, Gilbert 122
De Cárdenas, Raúl 22
De Castro Sisters, The 87
de Córdova, Pedro 83
Deedy, Carmen 65

De La Cruz, Miguel A. 222
del Castillo, Isora 118
De Rojas de la Portilla,
Agustín 140
Díaz-Oliver, Remedios 131
Domínguez, Jorge I. 227
Dosal, Margarita 123

**E**

Echevarría, René 73

Estévez, Felipe 160

**F**

Fanjul, Alfonso "Alfy" 135
Fanjul, José 'Pepe" 135
Fernández Cavada, Adolfo
242
Fernández Cavada, Federico
242
Fernández, Esteban 21
Fernández, Luis 212
Fernández, Miguel "Mike"
130

Fernández, Nohema 215
Fernández-Rundle, Katherine
253
Fernández-Valle, Cristina 201
Fernández-Vázquez, Antonio
161
Ferro, Pablo 62
Firmat, Francisco 153
Fusco, Coco 68

**G**

Gallegos, Luisa 118
Garazi, Solomon 121
García, Adriano 255
García-Eckstein, Ledy 152
García, Luis T. 169
García, Pedro E. 185

Gascón, George 247
Gil, Lourdes 163
Giménez, Carlos A. 257
Goico, Mario 190
Gómez, Pedro 37
Gonzáles, Ambrose E. 43

Gonzáles, N.G. 43
González, Edith 237
González, Flora 168
González, Manny 201

González-Torres, Félix 29
Gracia, Jorge J. E. 224
Guerra, Yalil 77

**H**

Halloran, María Cristina 165
Hernández, Horacio 82
Hernández, Luis A. 167

Hernández Valero, María de
Los Ángeles 157

**I**

Illing, Vivian Lousie 27

Isasi-Díaz, Ada María 198

**J**

Jerez, Magali 161

**K**

Kennedy, Rosario 250

**L**

Lámelas, Joseph 204
Larramendi Blakely, Lara 259
Larrañaga, Jim 106
Le Batard, Dan 47
León, Luis 183
Levy, William 93

Lima, Robert 218
Llorens, Hugo 147
Lochte, Ryan 114
López, Melinda 48
Loren, Josie 79
Lowinger, Rosa 127

**M**

Machado, Gus 132
Magill, Ron 56
Marill, Alicia 255
Marrero, Mirtha 118
Martínez, Aldo 175
Martínez, Hilarión 176
Martínez, Lorenzo Pablo 151
Martin, Frank 116
Mayorkas, Alejandro 256
Mayor, Mireya 194
Maza, Elena 150

McHale, Christina 115
Membiela, Roymi 57
Mendieta, Ana 148
Menéndez, Joe 64
Merediz, Olga 67
Meruelo, Alex 128
Mir, Frank 115
Miro, José E. 246
Montaner, Carlos Alberto 13
Moreno, Jorge 86

## N

Nespral, Jackie 80

Nin, Anaís 92

## O

Oliva, Erneido 251
Ordoñez, Ray 102

Ortega, Ralph 105

## P

Pascual, Camilo 99
Pascual, Carlos 239
Pérez-Farfante, Isabel 205

Pérez, Migdalia 118
Pérez, Rudy 75
Portes, Alejandro 217

## R

Rabassa, Gregory 228
Rassler, Amarilys 180
Ratner, Brett 71
Reinhart, Carmen 211
Reyes, Manolo 34
Riveron, Alberto 117
Rizo, Marco 54
Robreno, Eduardo C. 184
Rodríguez, Amy 109
Rodríguez, Eduardo D. 203

Rodríguez, Graciliano 135
Rodríguez, Marcos 129
Rodríguez-Nogues, Lourdes 162
Rodríguez, Rodri 145
Rodríguez, Santiago 139
Rubio, Carlos 166
Ruiz, Gloria 118
Ruiz, Teófilo F. 225
Rumbaut, Rubén 220

## S

Sacre, Antonio 49
Sánchez, María Dolores 235
Sánchez, Mario Ernesto 178
Sánchez, Nicolás 172
Sánchez, Ralph 188
San Juan, Miguel 158
Sanmartín, Cecilia 77
Sarria, Luis 104
Seinuk, Ysrael 208
Senarens, Luis P. 79

Serrano, Amy 45
Sigler, Vicente 19
Silva, John Henry 210
Siu, Albert 207
Sosa, Ernest 200
Sosa, Marta 33
Suárez, Virgil 216
Suchlicki, Jaime 231
Szapocznik, José 191

## T

Tanakeyowma, Lilia 181
Torres, Dara 111

Torres, Tico 81
Triay, Mike 52

# V

Valladares, Armando  259
Valls, Felipe  126
Vega, Matías G.  192
Vélez, María Teresa  154
Versalles, Zoilo  103
Vialat, Zonia  118
Viera, Ricardo  155
Viera, Yusnier  229
Visiedo, Octavio  177
Vizcaíno, María Argelia  95

Made in the USA
Lexington, KY
17 May 2017